Discover the SAVAGE WORLD

Contributors:

Simon Adams

Camilla de la Bedoyere

Ian Graham

Steve Parker

Phil Steele

Clint Twist

Discovery CHANNEL™

Miles Kelly

CONTENTS

First published in 2013 by
Miles Kelly Publishing Ltd
Harding's Barn, Bardfield End Green,
Thaxted, Essex, CM6 3PX, UK

This edition published in 2014

10 9 8 7 6 5 4 3 2 1

Publishing Director Belinda Gallagher
Creative Director Jo Cowan
Managing Editor Amanda Askew
Managing Designer/Cover Designer Simon Lee
Senior Editors Carly Blake, Rosie Neave
Designers Simon Lee, D&A Design,
   Rocket Design (East Anglia) Ltd, Tall Tree Ltd
Assistant Editor Amy Johnson
Proofreader Fran Bromage
Image Manager Liberty Newton
Production Manager Elizabeth Collins
Reprographics Stephan Davis, Thom Allaway,
   Anthony Cambray, Jennifer Hunt

ISBN 978-1-78209-496-8

Printed in China

British Library Cataloging-in-Publication Data
A catalog record for this book is available
from the British Library

Made with paper from a sustainable forest

www.mileskelly.net
info@mileskelly.net

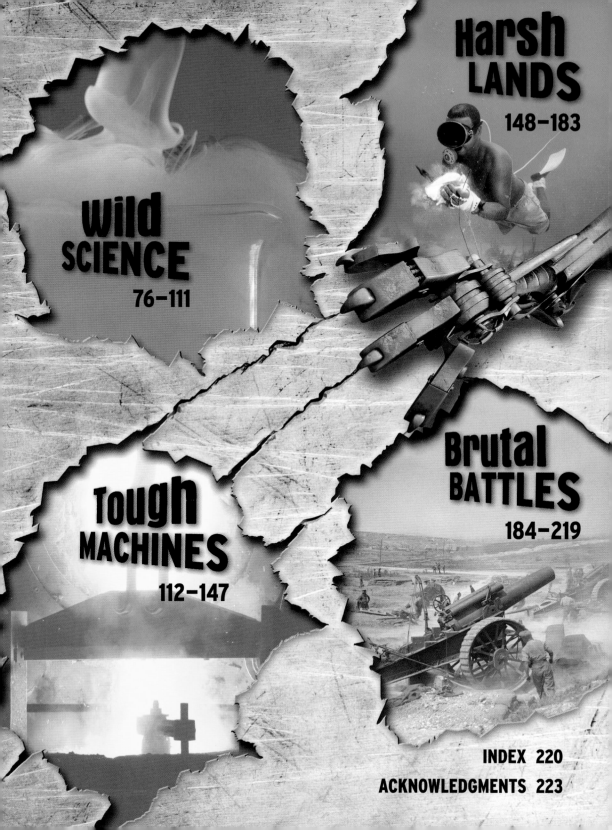

Earth's POWER

From tornadoes that tear up the land to earthquakes that burn it to cinders, find out about the fierce natural forces that wreak havoc on our planet.

◄ Lightning strikes as a gigantic supercell storm looms over South Dakota, U.S., creating an eerily dramatic display.

Early ERUPTIONS

A large volcanic eruption is massive, sudden, and savage. It shakes the ground, raining molten lava and ash over a vast area. Today, such an eruption only occurs every 10 or 20 years. But just after Earth formed, much of the world was in volcanic turmoil.

▼ Earth formed as small fragments of rock stuck together. The protoplanet grew quickly in size and also formed an atmosphere.

◄ Early planets, called protoplanets, formed when their gravitational forces collected surrounding rock and dust.

From dust we came

Long ago, a supernova exploded causing a shockwave that disturbed a giant dust-gas cloud. This cloud started to spin, then condensed, compressing into lumps. The central bulge became the fiery Sun and the outer chunks formed planets. By 4,500 million years ago, the Solar System had formed.

| 4,400 mya Earth begins to cool. Water is present | 4,000 mya Oldest-known rocks are from this period | 4,100–3,800 mya Earth is bombarded by asteroids and meteorites | 3,500 mya Possible signs of life | 3,000 mya Good evidence of life |

▼ Fierce rainstorms lasted for thousands of years, as floods and giant waves shaped the early land.

EARTH'S EARLY ATMOSPHERE CONTAINED MANY DEADLY GASES.

Boiling rocks

Early Earth was a hellish place. As gases and dust collapsed under the pressure of their own increasing gravity, they became hot rocks. Volcanoes covered huge areas and erupted for millions of years. Poisonous fumes and ashes spurted from the surface, and glowing rivers of rock flooded from cracks and vents. The enormous heat and toxic atmosphere meant that no life could survive.

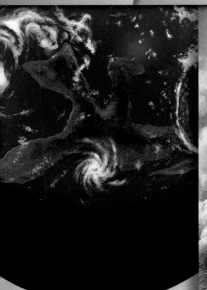

Violent birth

Chunks of matter circling the Sun attracted other lumps and grew into several protoplanets, one being Earth. It was a time of colossal impacts as space debris knocked these bodies around, added to them, or smashed lumps out of them. As the protoplanets rotated, they took on spherical (ball-like) shapes.

Sea fury

As the planet cooled, volcanic vapors condensed into liquid water. More water may have formed during the Late Heavy Bombardment, a time of repeated meteorite and asteroid smashes that vaporized on impact. The new water trickled down rocky slopes and pooled as seas and oceans. It was still hot, and the rocks steamed. Slowly the savage conditions subsided and temperatures calmed. In water, early microbes appeared. The era of life began.

BLOWING
its Top

Some volcanoes ooze and spit every day. Others have months or years between bursts. Mount St. Helens had been dormant for many years before it erupted in March 1980, wreaking havoc on the U.S. state of Washington and the 11 surrounding states. But what was it like to be there?

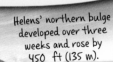

March 20

Our geological team arrived near Mount St. Helens after a 90-mi (145-km) trip south from Seattle. Reports of small tremors for several days now. Two days ago a Richter 4.1 'quake shook the flank. After more than 120 years, dormant "Helen" is waking up.

Helens' northern bulge developed over three weeks and rose by 450 ft (135 m).

The team collected vapor samples from vents to analyze for sulfur dioxide and other component gases.

March 27

We've set up seismometers, theodolites, and other equipment. Two huge geyserlike spurts of steam, ash, vapor, and rock erupted with fearsome noise. The existing summit crater has developed a smaller parasitic crater 250 ft (76 m) across. Further preshocks shake the area.

March 30

Small tremors occur every few minutes. Another parasitic crater has appeared. Outgassings—trapped gas released from the ground—ignited by lava brighten the night sky. A storm produced massive lightning bolts that flickered through ash clouds.

April 29

Triangulation readings using slope angles show the north side of the mountain bulges by 250 ft (76 m) and grows 6 ft (2 m) every day, due to internal pressure from rising magma. Hundreds of tremors daily.

March 1980

Tuesday	Wednesday	Thursday	Friday	Saturday
				1
4	5	6	7	8
11	12	13	14	15
18	19	20 ✳	21	22
25	26 ✳	27	28	29

May 23

It's five days after the primary eruption, heard more than 200 mi (320 km) away. Readings show the mountain is 1,300 ft (400 m) lower. Aircraft monitoring indicates the ash cloud rose to 10,000 ft (3,000 m), visible for hundreds of miles. Ash is falling 2,000 mi (3,200 km) away.

Blasted by Helens' force, stripped logs lie like matchsticks on nearby Spirit Lake, which rose by 200 ft (60 m).

BREAKING NEWS
MAY 18, 1980: MOUNT ST. HELENS ERUPTS!

Just after 8.30 p.m. seismometers almost went off the scale. Helens' north side blasted apart. A massive outpouring of lava, like a gigantic landslide, traveled at 150 mph (240 km/h) and left a path of slurry, rocks, and debris more than 17 mi (27 km) long. Seismic activity peaked at 3 pm. With pressure released, pyroclastic flows—superheated clouds of ash, rock particles, and gases—scorched an area 25 mi (40 km) wide and 20 mi (32 km) long. Glaciers melted and lahars (large mudflows) mixed in, flowing for almost 50 mi (80 km).

The Daily News

HELENS' AFTERMATH

57 deaths!

200 homes and buildings destroyed!

180 mi (290 km) of roads gone!

More than 250 sq mi (650 sq km) burned to cinders!

BLANKETS OF ASH COVER THE SURFACE—HOW ARE YOU GETTING AROUND?

Yet in weeks plants sprouted, and in months many animals were back!

ANGRY Oceans

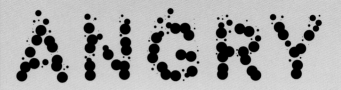

Water is heavy—15 bathtubs of water weigh as much as a family saloon car. On the move, this water has immense destructive power. Seawater is always moving as tides, currents, whirlpools, waterspouts, and storm surges.

▼ In the Bay of Fundy, Canada, the tidal range exceeds 59 ft (18 m). At low tide, fishing boats are grounded. Only five hours later, at high tide, water fills the harbor.

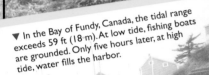

River wave

Tidal bores or "traveling waves" need a tidal range—the difference between high and low tide—of more than 20 ft (6 m). This allows the rising water to funnel into a narrow, shallow river and push against the flow. The tallest bore in the world is on Qiantang River, China. It's 30 ft (9 m) high and races along at 25 mph (40 km/h). The 7-ft (2-m) bore on England's Severn River benefits from a huge tidal range of almost 50 ft (15 m).

◄ March 2010's Severn bore attracted surfers from around the world.

Relentless tides

The rise and fall of the tides comes from the interplay of gravity from the Moon and Sun, combined with Earth's 24-hour spin. Tidal range increases where water piles up in long bays or estuaries. Both Canada's Bay of Fundy and Ungava Bay have extreme tidal ranges, more than 53 ft (16 m)—enough to cover a four-story building.

IN A SWIRL

Tides and currents create fierce ocean whirlpools. When adjacent tidal waters flow at different speeds or in opposite directions, they "rub edges," and spin. Massive whirlpools, or maelstroms, are 150 ft (46 m) across with waves curling 3 ft (one meter) tall. Despite legend, there is little downward flow, so whirlpools do not sink ships.

▼ Japan's 2011 tsunami caused major whirlpools, hundreds of feet wide, off the coast.

WATERSPOUTS—TORNADOES OVER WATER—CAN BE UP TO 330 FT (100 M) ACROSS AND 5,000 FT (1,500 M) TALL, WITH WINDS UP TO 250 FT/S (76 M/S).

THE FLOW OF WATER IN THE SALTSTRAUMEN MAELSTROM, NORWAY, PEAKS AT 40 MPH (64 KM/H).

Water surge

Storms can generate such strong winds along low coasts, they pile up seawater and blow it onto the land. When water is funneled into a bay, the effects are extreme. In 1899, Tropical Cyclone Mahina's winds drove a surge of water 45 ft (14 m) tall onto Bathurst Bay, northeast Australia. More than 300 people died. Seawater flooded the land, leaving behind salt that destroyed the land's ability to grow plants for many years.

▼ In 2007, storm surges threatened strong sea defenses in Scheveningen, the Netherlands.

Vanishing coasts

Even the hardest rocks succumb to unrelenting waves smashing and grinding them away, century after century. A soft-rock coastline can be swept aside in just one stormy night. In a few seconds, a headland collapse takes with it the buildings on top.

▼ In Port Campbell National Park, Victoria, Australia, the waves have eroded the soft sedimentary limestone to form a natural arch.

Graceful arches

Currents and wave action may scrape holes near the end of a headland, leaving a curve, the 160-ft- (50-m-) high Azure Window arch is the island of Malta, for many movies. Pieces regularly fall off and spectacular location for completely gone in 20 years. the whole arch may be

SLOW GRIND

Erosion eats soft rocks. Off the barrier reef rocks. U.S., the barrier of this coast of Louisiana, as much as 60 ft (18 m) faster than harder by as much as the end of this islands disappear will be gone by the sea consumes farmland, each year. The advancing sea consumes east coast, century, whole towns. On England's thousands of villages, of Dunwich in the 1280s washed the inhabitants. Storms in the town, with steady away half the erosion since. Fewer than 100 people live there now.

Land vs. sea

Coastal erosion is the wearing away of land by wind, tides, and waves. The severity of erosion depends on a number of factors—type and hardness of the rock, shoreline height and contours, prevailing wind speed, angle of water currents, and the likelihood of storms. One of the main problems is undercutting, where waves erode tall land at sea level, leaving the rock above ready to collapse.

▲ Large storm waves pick up sand, pebbles, and boulders and hurl them at the rock face, slowly undercutting a cliff in Corsica, France.

Disappearing islands

Islands are vanishing for a number of reasons. The islet of Surtsey, near Iceland, appeared when a submerged volcano poked above the waves in 1963. It grew until 1967, and now erosion is causing it to shrink. Some islands are sinking because the tectonic plates—giant curved slabs of rock that form Earth's crust—are gradually descending into Earth's mantle. Increasingly a major culprit is global warming, which expands water in the oceans, and also causes icy regions to melt and therefore sea levels to rise.

▲ Coastal erosion washes away sand and soil where trees once grew, uprooting and killing them.

IN NOVEMBER 2010, HURRICANE TOMAS STRUCK THE CARIBBEAN. CLIFF COLLAPSES AT SOUFRIÈRE, ST. LUCIA, MADE MORE THAN 5,000 PEOPLE HOMELESS.

Sand BLASTED

It begins as a vague haze on the horizon. The advancing wall of boiling sand and dust never seems to come into focus, but gets bigger and roars louder. Then suddenly—brown-out. You can hardly see your hands, but you don't want to look. The whipping particles sting your eyes, flay your ears, assault your nostrils, and choke your throat. Time to take cover.

▼ In 2009, red outback soil blew into Sydney, Australia, forcing people indoors and a transport shutdown.

Dusty city

In southwest U.S., sandstorms and dust storms are common in summer when a wind shift brings moisture-laden subtropical air from the south. This triggers thunderstorms with downbursts that kick up the desert's thin soil. Phoenix, Arizona, is regularly menaced by dusty 60-mph (96-km/h) winds that smother people, traffic, aircraft, and air-conditioners.

Rapid spread

A haboob is a small, powerful, concentrated dust storm caused by a clustered mass of cool, heavy air moving along within a region of warm air. It occurs when storm clouds break up and sink to the ground as downbursts, fragmenting into several horizontal flows. Haboobs affect dry places such as the Sahara desert, Middle East, Central Australia, and southwest North America. They happen fast and their winds reach 60 mph (96 km/h), but usually pass in a few minutes.

▶ Following an especially dry spring, a summer "dusty" rolls in from the parched surrounds to suffocate downtown Phoenix, U.S.

The right ingredients

Sandstorms and dust storms need two ingredients to start. The first is loose dry particles, usually in an arid region with extra weeks of no rain, shrunken rivers, and a lowered groundwater level. The second is updraft winds, generally from a large block of dry, cool air that warms and rises as it moves over hot ground. The winds lift the particles so they bounce along, breaking into smaller, lighter pieces that float more easily.

▶ Satellites track a giant dust storm hundreds of miles wide, stretching from northeast Africa to the Arabian Peninsula.

IN 2012 A SUDDEN DUST STORM IN RIYADH, SAUDI ARABIA, TURNED DAY INTO NIGHT—VEHICLE AND BUILDING LIGHTS CAME ON AT ONLY 4 P.M.

SLOW-MOTION SAVAGERY

Sandstorms and dust storms are part of long-term desertification. In dry regions, overgrazing by farm animals and too many crops using poor agriculture exhaust the soil, turning it dusty. Drought worsens the problem. In North Africa's Sahel, south of the Sahara, there are 100 days of sandstorms each year, and the human-made "desert" advances by up to 5 mi (8 km).

▲ During one of Kenya's regular droughts, farm workers flee as a dust storm sweeps past. The livestock are malnourished and farms struggle to survive.

Cover up!

When a sandstorm warning goes out, people prepare fast. The wind drives tiny grains through the smallest gaps and cracks, so that one small draft leaves everything inside coated with fine dust. Cover must be sought. Valuable items such as cars, tractors, wells, and irrigation vents are protected; and doors, shutters, windows, and other openings are closed and sealed.

▶ In the city of Turpan, northwest China, residents continue with their day whilst wearing masks to avoid inhaling the dust.

Fire! Fire!

An uncontrollable fire breaks out in the countryside, devouring the vegetation. A wildfire has begun. Wildfires can be the result of natural causes—lightning strikes, volcanic lava and ash, sparks from rockfalls, and even the Sun's rays focused through natural clear crystals. Nowadays, human error is also a major factor.

◄ On East Africa's vast grasslands, animals such as gazelles are used to outrunning the fast-approaching bushfires.

▲ To make a firebreak, firefighters pour flaming fuel from driptorches on the ground.

Part of nature

Wildfires are natural seasonal events in regions such as the East African savanna, American prairie, and Central Australian bush. Each year the dry period breaks as thunderstorms sweep in. Lightning torches the tinder-dry grass and scrub, and winds fan the flames. The flare-ups are rapid and fierce, but they soon fade as the rainy season gets underway.

Fighting fire

Modern firefighting has many methods to tackle big blazes. Vegetation can be prehosed to make it damp and less likely to catch. In areas at regular risk, firefighters often light small-scale burns to create open gaps called firebreaks. Finally, helicopters and "super-scooper" planes drop water to douse the flames.

▼ In Bunyip State Park, near Melbourne, Australia, the fire service monitors the spread of an enormous fire, with smoke filling the sky.

BLACK SATURDAY

One of Australia's worst tragedies began on February 7, 2009. In the southern state of Victoria, after two dry months, the temperature soared above 110°F (43°C) and winds gusted at 60 mph (96 km/h). More than 400 bushfires flared up, with causes ranging from sparking power lines to careless campfires. More fires broke out over the following three weeks. The final toll was 173 human deaths, dozens of towns destroyed, and huge areas of land scorched.

▼ Just three months after Australia's "Black Saturday," tree ferns in the hills of Victoria state were already extending their delicate new fronds.

▼ Firefighters nervously watch the wind direction in a raging central Californian forest fire.

Whipped by wind

High winds fan flames and make a fire spread at speeds of 15 mph (24 km/h) or more. Steady wind direction gives firefighters a chance to predict the burn area and make preparations. Sudden wind changes can alter the fire's route, trapping people and vehicles. In 2012, six firefighters died when a blaze near Carahue, Southern Chile, changed direction.

Black to green

Plants and animals cope well with natural wildfires. Trees have thick bark, grass roots are safe underground, and herbs make heat-resistant seeds that germinate after scorching. Animals hide underground, take flight, or flee. As the flames die down, shoots sprout up. In a few weeks, the blackened carpet turns green and life returns.

TSUNAMI!

PETER JONES Tohoku, Japan   LIVE

At 2.46 p.m. local time, a colossal earthquake shook Tohoku, the northern region of Japan's main island, Honshu. Giant waves are forecast to hit the closest shoreline within 30 minutes. Depending on seabed and coastal contours, some waves can reach 120 ft (35 m) high and surge more than 6 mi (10 km) inland. They are likely to flood huge areas of coastline.

THE CAUSE

Tsunami swell

Wave hits land

Earthquake's focus

Tectonic plates moving
one beneath another

The earthquake that triggered the tsunami was a megathrust event—two tectonic plates forming Earth's crust slipped, forcing one above the other. Scientists estimate its origin as 41 mi (66 km) east of Tohoku's coast and 20 mi (32 km) below the surface. The event lasted for six minutes and caused parts of the seabed to shift sideways by 160 ft (50 m) and rise up 20 ft (6 m). This shift pushed the water above, setting off the tsunami.

A FEW HOURS LATER

The rushing water carried everything in its path. Boats, cars, trucks, and trains were swept along like toys. Houses, offices, and factories were smashed to pieces in seconds. Hundreds of miles of roads, railroad lines, drainage systems, and other infrastructure were destroyed.

THREE DAYS LATER

An explosion occured at the Fukushima Nuclear Power Plant on the coast hit by flooding. The earthquake's tremors triggered auto-shutdown. However, the floods immobilized the reactor's cooling system, causing potential nuclear meltdown. People within 12 mi (20 km) were immediately evacuated.

Flash! BOOM!

Severe thunderstorms are some of Earth's most vicious events. Every second around the world, more than 2,000 places are under towering clouds, suffering torrential rain, huge hailstones, and violent winds. Thunderstorms cause great damage and destruction, leaving behind a shattered landscape.

The mothership

The biggest thunderstorms come from massive atmospheric features called supercells, which can be 50 mi (80 km) across and 12 mi (20 km) high. They form where warm air collides with cold air. Winds make the warm air rise and spin, gradually tilting upright with swirling updrafts inside.

▶ A storm hit South Dakota on July 23, 2010, bringing with it a giant supercell that poured record-breaking hailstones onto the area. The hailstones measured 8 in (20 cm) in diameter.

Ups and downs

As it rises, water vapor cools, causing it to condense and even freeze. During a thunderstorm, this produces towering cumulonimbus "anvil" clouds. Inside the clouds, water droplets are moved around in a cycle—rising, combining, falling, and then rising again. Eventually these icy balls may cause a heavy fall of hail or snow.

▼ A space station view 250 mi (400 km) high shows giant cumulonimbus over West Africa. The cloud flattened and spread out as it hit a natural barrier along the base of the stratosphere.

Stones of ice

Water vapor is blown to the top of a thunderstorm by updrafts of more than 100 mph (160 km/h). Here the temperature is many degrees below freezing. The drops eventually fall and thaw, merging together before being caught in an updraft again. This is how hailstones grow. The biggest exceed 8 in (20 cm) and weigh up to 2 lb (one kg).

▼ In June 2012, hailstones larger than tennis balls dented and smashed vehicles in Dallas.

Ash and flash

Lightning is caused by a build up of electrical charges in a cloud. The positive charges are near the cloud's top and the negative are lower down. The difference in charges becomes so great that finally a giant spark leaps to even them out—lightning. This instantly heats the air around it, forming a shock wave that spreads out like a sonic boom—thunder.

▶ Lightning appears in the plume of ash above the Chaiten volcano in southern Chile during the 2008 eruption. Scientists are unsure what causes a volcanic electrical storm.

AN AVERAGE LIGHTNING BOLT...

⚡ has enough electrical energy to power a typical household for one week

⚡ has an electrical "push" of more than 1,000 million volts. Domestic supply is 112–120 v (220–240 v)

⚡ has a temperature of 55,000°F (30,500°C)—eight times hotter than the Sun's surface

⚡ measures 1–2 mi (1.6–3.2 km) in length

⚡ has a flow of electricity, or current, of more than 250,000 amps. A low-energy lightbulb is less than 0.1 amps

Winds of
DESTRUCTION

Many atmospheric events cause the mass movement of air. Extreme winds often whip up as warm air clashes with cold air—resulting in a furious battle that inflicts devastation on the land below and creates havoc for planes in the sky.

DOWNBURSTS MORE THAN 2.5 MI (4 KM) ACROSS ARE KNOWN AS MACROBURSTS; SMALLER ONES ARE KNOWN AS MICROBURSTS.

Straight-line damage

A derecho is a widespread, fast-moving band of damaging straight-line winds and clusters of savage thunderstorms. Winds span more than 250 mi (400 km), persist for at least six hours, and reach a speed of at least 58 mph (93 km/h). Within the derecho are storms, rain, hail, and sudden wind currents called downbursts.

▲ Microbursts occur when air suddenly becomes colder in a thundercloud, causing an air column to move rapidly downward. If the air was wet, the microburst is joined by rainfall.

▲ A squall line—band of severe thunderstorms— can produce a derecho.

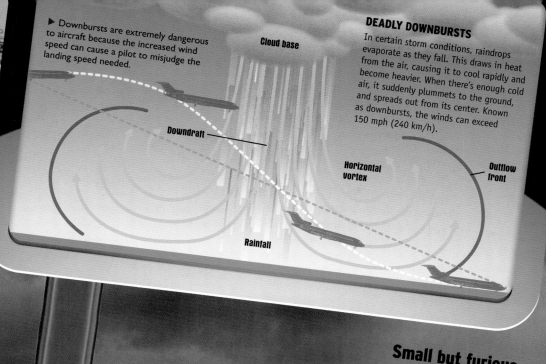

▶ Downbursts are extremely dangerous to aircraft because the increased wind speed can cause a pilot to misjudge the landing speed needed.

Cloud base

Downdraft

Horizontal vortex

Rainfall

Outflow front

DEADLY DOWNBURSTS

In certain storm conditions, raindrops evaporate as they fall. This draws in heat from the air, causing it to cool rapidly and become heavier. When there's enough cold air, it suddenly plummets to the ground, and spreads out from its center. Known as downbursts, the winds can exceed 150 mph (240 km/h).

Small but furious

Lasting just a couple of minutes, the ferocious 150-mph (240-km/h) winds of a microburst can cause as much destruction as a tornado—so people can confuse the two. However, there is a key difference between them. A tornado leaves behind a rotating pattern because winds spin around a center that moves along. Microburst winds blow out in straight lines from the center, causing damage in a radial pattern, like wheel spokes.

▼ The buran occurs often in Mongolia, with winds full of snow and ice, making it difficult for workers to get around.

Relentless blizzards

The buran or "blizzard wind" is a regular fierce airflow, usually from the northeast, that scours Central Asia. In summer, it brings duststorms. In winter, it carries blizzards of snow and ice, at temperatures below -20°F (-28°C). A typical buran blows at more than 35 mph (55 km/h) for several hours, and the snow reduces visibility to 300 ft (90 m) or less.

Mega monsoons

I n South Asia, the fiery sun heats the land and air over it, faster than the ocean. The hot air rises, and cooler, moist air flows in from the sea as the onshore monsoon wind. The monsoon season has arrived—months of Earth's wettest weather.

Looming danger

Monsoons are caused by seasonal changes in the direction of the wind. Warm, moist air blows in from the Indian Ocean toward southern Asian countries such as Pakistan, India, Bangladesh, and Burma. The air rises over the sunbaked land, then condenses as colossal amounts of rain. Heavy rains usually fall from June to September, starting in South Asia and then spreading to Southeast Asia and Australia.

▼ The first sign of the monsoon's arrival is large rainclouds looming on the horizon.

Pakistan suffers

Beginning in late July 2010, the heaviest monsoon rains for decades inundated Pakistan. Intense torrents over hills cascaded to the lowlands, breaking riverbanks and saturating farms, towns, and villages. By mid-August one fifth of the whole nation was flooded, 20 million people were displaced, and nearly 2,000 had died.

▼ People wade through deep water in an attempt to salvage their belongings after torrential rains caused floods in Pakistan in 2010.

IN JULY 2005, MORE THAN 64 IN (163 CM) OF RAIN FELL IN 36 HOURS ON INDIA'S CITY OF MUMBAI—MORE THAN NEW YORK CITY'S YEARLY RAINFALL.

◀ Children play in storm drains as monsoon rains bring relief from intense summer heat.

Coping with the deluge

Monsoons are regular annual events, and generally the land and the people cope. Storm drains, irrigation channels, road conduits, and other infrastructure are designed to handle the deluges. People also watch out for aquatic animals such as crocodiles that get caught in the flowing water.

SO MUCH RAIN

City	Average annual precipitation
Mawsynram, India	467 in (1,187 cm)
Brazzaville, Congo	73 in (185 cm)
Sydney, Australia	48 in (122 cm)
New York City, U.S.	47 in (119 cm)
Rio de Janeiro, Brazil	43 in (110 cm)
Beijing, China	25 in (63 cm)
London, England	24 in (61 cm)
Los Angeles, U.S.	15 in (38 cm)
Riyadh, Saudi Arabia	4 in (10 cm)

Huge HOLES

One minute the ground is there. Next, there's a great hole. Not all sinkholes form this quickly, but they are a regular feature in some landscapes and can also occur where humans have worked underground.

▼ In 2007, a 330-ft- (100-m-) deep hole formed under Guatemala City, central America. It was caused by sewage water leaking down through loose soil and old volcanic ash.

Look out below!

Sinkholes, swallowholes, and similar openings usually develop in certain kinds of rock such as limestone, dolomite, or sandstone. Underground rivers gradually erode a hidden cavity or cavern. The cavern gets so big that its roof is no longer supported and caves in.

▲ The Daisetta sinkhole reached an estimated 1,300 ft (400 m) across and 200 ft (60 m) deep.

Bigger and bigger

Some sinkholes start small and grow. At Daisetta, in Texas, U.S., a sinkhole appeared in May 2008. It swallowed trees and vehicles and continued to enlarge, at one stage by 20 ft (6 m) per hour, until it reached 600 ft (180 m) across and 150 ft (45 m) deep. It may have resulted from the collapse of a salt dome—a lump of salt, less dense than surrounding rock, that collected under the crust.

SUDDEN SINKHOLE

On February 28, 2013, a 60-ft (18-m) sinkhole opened up under a house in Florida, swallowing a bedroom. One person was killed as the ground crumbled away. Beneath Florida is a system of limestone caverns, eroded by water, causing them to collapse.

▲ After the house in Florida was demolished, the sinkhole was shown to threaten neighboring properties.

THE NOW-FLOODED LITTLE SALT SPRING SINKHOLES, IN FLORIDA, HAVE PRESERVED 6,500-YEAR-OLD HUMAN REMAINS AND A 13,500-YEAR-OLD PREHISTORIC GIANT TORTOISE.

Heavenly pits

"Tiankeng" is Chinese for "heavenly pit" and the name given to sinkholes at least 330 ft (100 m) deep and wide. Xiaozhai Tiankeng is the world's biggest, more than 2,160 ft (660 m) deep, with a mouth 2,030 ft (620 m) wide. Smaller holes appear regularly, such as the one that almost consumed Qingquan primary school in Dachegnqiao, near Changsha, southeast China in June 2010.

▼ The Qingquan hole grew to 500 ft (150 m) wide and 150 ft (45 ft) deep, destroying or undermining 30 dwellings.

Falling DOWN

It takes only a small movement to trigger a landslide or avalanche. Without warning, nature lets loose with a sudden, unstoppable mass movement that covers, smashes, and sweeps away everything in its path.

Savage slips

Landslips and landslides have various triggers, such as heavy rain, erosion, earthquakes, or even loose rock. Poor farming and forestry worsen the risks by removing plant cover from the ground. In December 1999, the state of Vargas, Venezuela, was ravaged by a series of landslips and mudslides after receiving 36 in (91 cm) of rain in three days. Up to 30,000 people died and 300,000 were made homeless.

▶ During Tropical Storm Talas in Japan, 2011, a sudden downpour loosened the soil on this steep slope. It was forced downhill, destroying buildings at the bottom.

WATCH FOR FALLEN ROCKS

Snow slide

When heavy snow piles up on a mountain slope, pressure can instigate the snow mass movement—new snowfall, an animal. The whoosh movement—a mountain animal. The mass movement, a kick from a loud sound, the fiercer melting, a kick from a slope, the 100 mph (160 km/h). In 1954 near Blons, Austria, two earth tremor, and even a slope, up to 100 mph (160 steeper and smoother the 100 mph. two the flow, traveling near Blons, Austria, killed km/h). In quick succession killed more than 200 people.

▶ Rescue workers check the forward edge of an avalanche that tumbled down a slope in the ski resort of Hinterstoder, Austria in April 2009.

Death clouds

A pyroclastic flow is an incredibly rapid, surging cloud of gas and particles superheated, often due to its partial collapse. As hot as 1,800°F (1,000°C), the flow cascades from a volcano, often over 400 mph downhill at speeds of more than 400 mph (640 km/h). It torches and burns everything in its path. During the 1990s in the Caribbean, parts of the island of Montserrat were overwhelmed by pyroclastic flows, lahars, and ashfalls.

▶ The Soufrière Hills Volcano, Montserrat, regularly belches out ash. This cloud followed the collapse of a small bulge on the main lava dome.

IN 1902, THE PYROCLASTIC FLOWS OF MOUNT PELÉE, ON THE CARIBBEAN ISLAND OF MARTINIQUE, KILLED UP TO 30,000 PEOPLE.

▲ Remote mountainous areas often suffer after heavy rain. A mudslide near Mianzhu, China, trapped 500 people in their homes.

▶ Areas where roads are cut into the rock along steep hillsides of scree (loose rocky fragments) are commonly hit by rockfalls.

Muddy mayhem

A lahar is a fast, hot mudflow from an erupting volcano. The sudden heat melts glaciers and snowfields. The sudden heat melts soil to form snowfields. The water mixes with slopes into valleys of debris that gushes down town of Amero, Colombia. In 1985 the lahars following the eruption of Nevado del Ruiz volcano, was engulfed by were lost. More than 20,000 lives

Rock block

Rockfalls occur when melting ice and snow liquify soil on steep slopes, allowing boulders to slip. These boulders tumble downhill, crashing into and moving any rocks in their path. Quickly the rockfall gains size and momentum.

29

TYPHOON TERROR

Thelma's survivors experience the stench of decay at a mass burial in Ormoc City.

Vast rotating swirls of air, usually centered around low-pressure winds spiraling inward, make deadly weather features. They have different names—hurricanes in the Atlantic and east Pacific, cyclones near India, and typhoons in the northwest Pacific, where the islands of the Philippines are often right in their path...

Typhoon Thelma, 1991

The Philippines is used to several typhoons each season. In October 1991, Thelma was not especially powerful, with winds peaking at 50 mph (80 km/h). But it was certainly devastating, causing more than 6,000 deaths. Immense rainfall flooded the land, with some areas receiving more then 20 in (50 cm) in 24 hours. On the central island of Leyte, many people died from drowning and landslides.

Typhoon Parma, 2009

A few days after Typhoon Ketsana hit the central Philippines in October 2009, Parma hurtled across its northern zone. Peak winds registered at more than 110 mph (175 km/h). The authorities ordered controlled opening of several dams, to avoid them overflowing or cracking under pressure—this meant evacuating thousands of homes. Water transport, from fishing boats and ferries to huge cargo ships, was stopped. The total damage topped $6 million (£3.9 million), making it the Philippines' second costliest typhoon ever.

Parma's floods swept through many Philippine towns and cities, such as Santa Cruz.

1979'S TYPHOON TIP WAS 1,400 MI (2,250 KM) ACROSS WITH WINDS REACHING 190 MPH (305 KM/H).

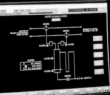

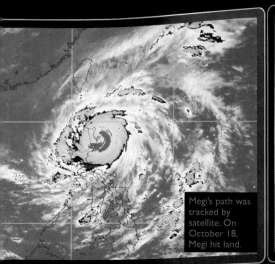

Megi's path was tracked by satellite. On October 18, Megi hit land.

Typhoon Washi, 2011

In December 2011, it was Washi's turn to blast the Philippines, dumping 8 in (20 cm) of rain in just a few hours and causing flash floods more than 3 ft (one meter) deep. Most of the 1,270-plus deaths were due to flooding, which swept away roads, power lines, bridges, and tunnels, and triggered landslides in hilly built-up areas.

Washi's flash floods tossed vehicles around, often into houses.

Typhoon Megi, 2011

Super-typhoons have wind speeds of more than 150 mph (240 km/h). In October 2010, Megi was the only super-typhoon of the Pacific season, with one blast measured at 185 mph (295 km/h). It made landfall on Luzon, Philippines, then pushed on to Taiwan and China. Total deaths were more than 70.

Aid workers dispense food rations in Calumpit, one of the worst-hit towns, in the Philippines.

Philippine police load relief supplies at Cauayan, north Philippines, to airlift south to worst-hit areas.

Typhoon Nesat-Nalgae, 2011

Within a week of each other in late September and early October 2011, typhoons Nesat and Nalgae killed more than 100 people in the Philippines. The first saturated the ground and set off floods; the second worsened an already dire situation. Nesat alone wrecked more than 45,000 houses, and some towns were cut off for more than 10 days.

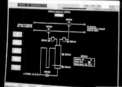

Haiti QUAKE

On January 12, 2010, the Caribbean nation of Haiti suffered a tremendous 7.0-magnitude earthquake, followed by two strong aftershocks of 5.9 and 5.5 magnitude. The effects were catastrophic—hundreds of thousands were killed and injured and the reconstruction costs are estimated to be $11.5 billion (£7.4 billion).

▼ Haiti's earthquake occured along a strike-slip fault—a break in Earth's crust—where the two sides of the fault slide against each other.

I Tectonic plates are held in position by the friction between them.

2 Enough pressure builds to overcome this friction, releasing energy as destructive seismic waves.

▲ An aerial shot shows the extent of the damage two days after the main earthquake—downtown Port-Au-Prince was almost flattened.

The origin

The earthquake's center, or focus, was about 8 mi (13 km) underground, 15 mi (24 km) west of the nation's capital, Port-au-Prince. It happened as sections of the Caribbean and North American tectonic plates shifted against each other. The ground shook in some places for up to one minute, and the tremors could be felt as far away as Cuba, 500 mi (800 km) away.

The impact

Haiti is a poor nation, with shanty-town buildings and low-standard infrastructure. When the earthquake hit, the effect was disastrous. Many areas were completely flattened. Hospitals, transport, and communications were demolished. People struggled to survive, stranded outside, with little food and great risk of disease.

Rapid relief

A major earthquake destroys infrastructure and leaves people injured, hungry, and homeless. Within a few days international aid workers in Haiti organized essentials such as medicines, food, tents, and fuel.

▲ Haitians clamber aboard a ferry carrying food and medicine to the worst-hit areas of Port-au-Prince.

To the rescue

In several countries around the world, including the U.S., France, Britain, Germany, Japan and Australia, specialist teams of rescue workers are on standby. Within hours of a disaster, they are in action. They bring sophisticated equipment, such as sensors, which detect body heat, faint noises, and even carbon dioxide gas exhaled by people trapped in the rubble.

▼ Rescue workers in Port-au-Prince carefully carry a survivor from a collapsed building.

THE MOST POWERFUL RECORDED QUAKE WAS THE GREAT CHILEAN EARTHQUAKE OF MAY 1960, WITH A MAGNITUDE OF 9.5.

Immense toll

Due to a lack of civilian records, an accurate death toll is unknown. It is thought that 250,000 were killed and 300,000 injured. More than 100,000 homes were lost and thousands of other buildings destroyed. Two million were made homeless, forced to live in temporary shelters.

▼ Huge tent-and-tarpaulin cities were built to house the homeless. Poor sanitation meant that the people were at risk of disease such as cholera.

TWISTER CENTRAL

The world's fastest winds occur in some of its smallest weather features—tornadoes or "twisters." They can materialize almost anywhere, from northern Europe to south Africa, blowing at speeds of more than 125 mph (200 km/h). Some of the fiercest tornadoes ransack the U.S.'s Tornado Alley.

JET STREAM

Along the Alley

Tornado Alley runs from northwest Texas through Oklahoma and Kansas to Nebraska. This is the Great Plains—vast flats, with the Rocky Mountains to the west and Appalachians to the east. Along the Alley, dry, cold air from the Rockies and Canada to the north collides with warm, damp air from the Gulf of Mexico—perfect conditions to form twisters.

COLD DRY AIR

South Dakota

Nebraska

TORNADO ALLEY

Oklahoma

Narrow but total

Tornadoes in open farmland damage crops and hit small communities, with a lesser, yet serious, toll. Tracking through built-up areas leaves a long, narrow, intense strip of destruction—as with the twister that hit Joplin, Missouri, in May 2011. Its winds reached 200 mph (320 km/h), and more than 120 people were killed and more than 1,000 injured.

WARM DRY AIR

Texas

▼ An aerial view of a tornado's straight-line path, in Joplin, 2011.

MORE THAN 80 PERCENT OF TORNADOES OCCUR FROM APRIL TO JULY, BETWEEN 3 P.M. AND 7 P.M.

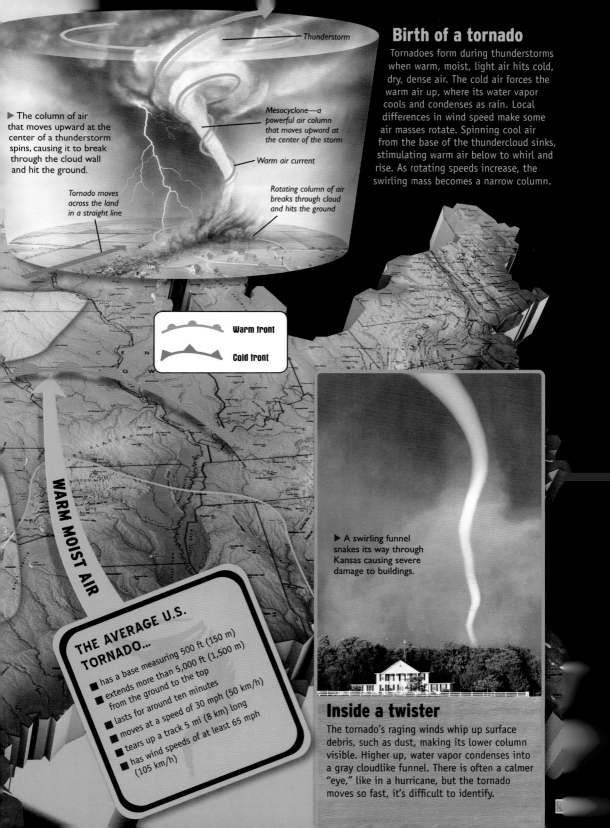

Thunderstorm

Birth of a tornado

Tornadoes form during thunderstorms when warm, moist, light air hits cold, dry, dense air. The cold air forces the warm air up, where its water vapor cools and condenses as rain. Local differences in wind speed make some air masses rotate. Spinning cool air from the base of the thundercloud sinks, stimulating warm air below to whirl and rise. As rotating speeds increase, the swirling mass becomes a narrow column.

▶ The column of air that moves upward at the center of a thunderstorm spins, causing it to break through the cloud wall and hit the ground.

Mesocyclone—a powerful air column that moves upward at the center of the storm

Warm air current

Tornado moves across the land in a straight line

Rotating column of air breaks through cloud and hits the ground

Warm front

Cold front

WARM MOIST AIR

▶ A swirling funnel snakes its way through Kansas causing severe damage to buildings.

THE AVERAGE U.S. TORNADO...

- ■ has a base measuring 500 ft (150 m)
- ■ extends more than 5,000 ft (1,500 m) from the ground to the top
- ■ lasts for around ten minutes
- ■ moves at a speed of 30 mph (50 km/h)
- ■ tears up a track 5 mi (8 km) long
- ■ has wind speeds of at least 65 mph (105 km/h)

Inside a twister

The tornado's raging winds whip up surface debris, such as dust, making its lower column visible. Higher up, water vapor condenses into a gray cloudlike funnel. There is often a calmer "eye," like in a hurricane, but the tornado moves so fast, it's difficult to identify.

TOO MUCH WATER

Water is vital for life—but too much drowns life, washes away homes, wrecks buildings and destroys roads. Floods are caused by a number of events—from too much rain and monsoon deluge to glaciers melting and earthquakes breaking riverbanks. In December 2010, Queensland, Australia, felt the full wrath of water's power.

▶ The walls of this house in Ipswich, near Brisbane, were submerged by 10 ft (3 m) of floodwater, leaving just the roof visible.

▼ La Niña occurs across the tropical Pacific Ocean about every five years, bringing extreme weather such as floods and droughts. It causes wetter conditions in Australia, Southern Africa, and Southeast Asia, and drier conditions along the coastal regions of Peru, Chile, and southern U.S.

ASIA

NORTH AMERICA

Polar jet stream

Pacific jet stream

AUSTRALASIA

SOUTH AMERICA

A series of causes

Queensland's floods had several probable causes. One was heavy, widespread, persistent rainfall from Cyclone Tasha. This shortlived, forceful storm surged in from the ocean and headed southwest into the state's interior.

Tasha coincided with the La Niña-El Niño cycle—La Niña returns every few years to "oppose" El Niño. It brings cool water temperatures to the ocean's southeast, which then pushes warm, moist, rain-bearing air toward Australia.

Some scientists believe climate change and global warming were also contributing factors. This may only be confirmed in another decade or two.

IN 1931, CHINA'S YELLOW RIVER UNLEASHED A DEVASTATING DELUGE THAT KILLED UP TO FOUR MILLION PEOPLE—THE WORLD'S WORST-EVER NATURAL DISASTER.

The Big Wet

From December 2010 until January 2011, Australia's northeast state of Queensland suffered mammoth floods. At their worst, the waters affected almost half the state, and the national authorities declared three quarters of Queensland a disaster zone. The torrent flooded coal mines and quarries, washed away roads and rail, and damaged houses and buildings—economic losses are estimated to be more than $11 billion (£7.2 billion).

Floods damage farmland too. This crop of sorghum near Toowoomba, Queensland, was wiped out.

Flash floods

Queensland's floods got off to a stuttering start in early December with greater-than-usual regular rainfall. Over the Christmas and New Year period, Cyclone Tasha arrived and the rains just kept coming. On January 9–10, 2011, more than 6 in (15 cm) fell in 36 hours on already soaked ground around Toowoomba. Water surged through the city, carrying away cars and trucks and leaving the city center in total ruin.

Brisbane under water

By January 11, 2011, floodwaters flowing east reached the city of Ipswich, near Queensland's capital, Brisbane. The Bremer River here rose nearly 65 ft (20 m). The water bulges continued and in Brisbane itself, its namesake Brisbane River went up 15 ft (4.6 m), swallowing 20,000 homes.

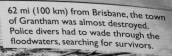

62 mi (100 km) from Brisbane, the town of Grantham was almost destroyed. Police divers had to wade through the floodwaters, searching for survivors.

Greatest ever?

Today's big floods are mere trickles compared to the Zanclean Deluge. Just over five million years ago, massive Earth movements opened a narrow channel, now the Strait of Gibraltar, which was then a vast, mostly dried-out basin. Within two years the Mediterranean refilled, sometimes rising 33 ft (10 m) daily, in perhaps the greatest flood the world has ever seen.

STORM OF THE CENTURY

NEWS

-5°C

EVERY FEW YEARS, A MAJOR STORM ATTACKS!

When certain conditions come together, the result is a "perfect storm" of immense size, power, and ferocity. One such storm occured in eastern North America during March 1993—the Storm of the Century.

Course of the storm

During early March 1993, low pressure over Mexico moved across the Gulf of Mexico toward Cuba and Florida. It happened to coincide with the jet stream—the high-altitude corridor of rushing air. Cold air was pulled from the far north as the storm tracked northeast over several days, along the Atlantic seaboard into Canada, before fading in late March. This perfect storm became known as the Storm of the Century (SOTC).

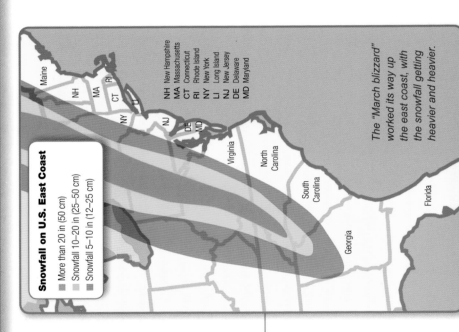

Snowfall on U.S. East Coast

- More than 20 in (50 cm)
- Snowfall 10–20 in (25–50 cm)
- Snowfall 5–10 in (12–25 cm)

Maine
NH
MA
CT RI
NY
LI
NJ
DE
MD
Virginia
North Carolina
South Carolina
Georgia
Florida

NH New Hampshire
MA Massachusetts
CT Connecticut
RI Rhode Island
NY New York
LI Long Island
NJ New Jersey
DE Delaware
MD Maryland

The "March blizzard" worked its way up the east coast, with the snowfall getting heavier and heavier.

SOTC STATS

* Other names: Great Blizzard of '93, Superstorm of '93, '93 Nor'easter.

* Date: March 11–16, 1993.

* Maximum snowfall (undrifted): 6 ft (1.8 m).

* Lowest atmospheric pressure: 960 mb.

* Maximum wind gust: Cuba 130 mph (210 km/h), United States 140 mph (225 km/h) on Mount Washington, New Hampshire.

* Boats lost: More than 300 reported but the actual toll was probably three times higher.

* On Long Island alone, 20 homes were lost to the sea due to huge waves.

* More than 150 people were rescued at sea by U.S. Coast Guard in the Gulf of Mexico and Atlantic.

* Electricity outages: Affected a total of more than 100 million people.

* Total volume of water falling as rain, snow, and hail was similar to 40 days of flow of the Mississippi River in New Orleans.

FROM TRAVEL PROBLEMS TO DESTROYED HOMES, THE SOTC AFFECTED MORE THAN ONE THIRD OF THE U.S. POPULATION.

HURRICANE SANDY STATS

🌀 In October 2012 Hurricane Sandy ravaged through the Caribbean and up the east coast of North America.

🌀 At its greatest, Sandy was classed as a category 3 hurricane and measured more than 1,000 mi (1,600 km) across.

🌀 Sandy hit Jamaica, Cuba, and the Bahamas, then moved north off the eastern seaboard to blast ashore in New Jersey.

🌀 In New York City, the storm surge caused power outages and flooding in road tunnels and subways.

🌀 Total damage is estimated at $80 billion (£50 billion), and the death toll close to 300.

HALLOWEEN NOR'EASTER

When conditions really come together, a "perfect storm" of truly exceptional size, power, and ferocity results. The 1991 Halloween Nor'Easter, which spun off Hurricane Grace, inspired the 1997 book and 2000 movie *The Perfect Storm*.

Blizzards aplenty

Average yearly snowfall in Birmingham, Alabama, is one inch (2.5 cm). The SOTC dumped 17 in (43 cm) on this unprepared city. Northeast states are used to winter snow, but the SOTC was late in the season and its blizzards broke records. Syracuse, New York, had a fall of 40 in (100 cm). Drifts near the Canadian border reached 35 ft (11 m).

Unprepared motorists became stranded in fierce blizzards.

Big freeze down south

Freezing temperatures hit almost everywhere. Birmingham went down to 2°F (-17°C), far from its March average of 54°F (12°C). High winds added to the havoc and more than ten tornadoes spun off the main storm system. Cuba experienced gusts of 130 mph (210 km/h). In Florida, blasts at more than 100 mph (160 km/h) caused storm surges along the coast of more than 12 ft (3.7 m).

Massive waves pound the shoreline near Tampa, Florida, on March 13, as the storm progressed northward.

Travel shutdown

As the SOTC moved north, it closed every airport in turn from Georgia to Nova Scotia. Hundreds of highways and thousands of smaller routes were blocked for days. The snow's weight brought down roofs in factories, sports centers, and shopping malls. Millions went without power, some for a week.

LaGuardia Airport, New York, was shut for almost two days, and took nearly another week to return to normal.

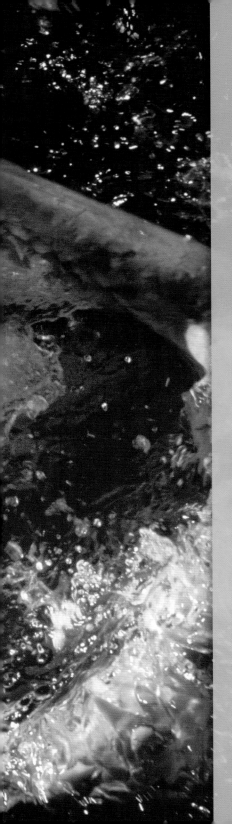

Deadly NATURE

Prepare to be scared—animals are ready to fight tooth and claw when it comes to the crunch, with weapons ranging from lethal toxins to electro-senses.

◀ A great white shark's gaping mouth, lined with daggerlike teeth, looms menacingly upward, ready to engulf potential prey.

Family FEUDS

Family life in the animal world is not all fun and games. There is plenty of motivation for family fights—competition for food is a common source of friction. However, relatives do have their uses, especially when it comes to uniting against a common enemy.

BIRD BRAWL

Given their tendency for violence toward one another, it's a wonder that mallards are one of the most widespread duck species. Life for ducklings is unusually precarious because adults often attack and kill any youngsters they encounter—and some mothers have been known to kill their own offspring in cases of mistaken identity. Drakes (male mallards) also attack each other at breeding time in belligerent battles over territory and mating rights.

A drake may attempt to drown its rival by pinning it below the water.

In Botswana, two bull heads as they attempt to long tusks in a fight for can be so ferocious that

African elephants smash spear each other with their supremacy. Sometimes fights tusks break.

CLASH OF THE TITANS

Brotherly love counts for nothing in an elephant family when it is mating time. Females lead the herds, so when males reach adulthood they are expelled and forced to roam the African plains. Bulls (male elephants) have a reputation as loners, but they often travel with brothers, cousins, or best friends until they come into musth, and their hormones take over. Musth is a frenzied time of fighting when male aggression levels soar, and kinship is forgotten in a competition for mates. It's a conflict that frequently results in serious injury or even death.

A cuckoo chick ejects its host's chick—a reed warbler—out of the nest, leaving just one mouth to feed—its own!

CUCKOOS IN THE NEST

Bringing up youngsters is risky. For animals, the reward is that their genes are passed onto the next generation. However, sometimes nature plays cruel tricks with caring parents. Cuckoos are brood parasites and lay their eggs in the nests of smaller birds. When the cuckoo chicks hatch, they push the host bird's chicks and eggs out of the nest. Unaware, the host parents continue to raise the cuckoo, which even imitates the "hungry" call of the host's own chicks.

Young fox cubs playfight with each other until they are around 16 weeks old.

BRINGING UP BABY

There are few animals more dangerous than a mother bear. Once her maternal instincts have been aroused, an adult female with a cub to protect can turn from docile to deadly in seconds. Undaunted by the size of an attacker, mothers will use claws and jaws to fight to the death. They usually only give up when they believe the attacker is dead.

A young brown bear cub looks on as its mother fights off an aggressive male.

Male elephants that are successful in their fights may be able to find as many as 30 mates in just one year, and could father as many calves.

SCHOOL OF HARD KNOCKS

The speed and accuracy required for survival are skills that can take a long time to master, so many youngsters playfight almost as soon as they can walk. Rough and tumble is accompanied by mock punches and gentle bites as siblings develop their hunting and defense strategies.

HISSING Killers

There are around 3,000 species of snake, and among them are some of the world's deadliest animals. These scaly serpents are equipped with one of the most dangerous natural substances on Earth—venom. Those that live near human habitations cause many deaths. The Indian Cobra alone accounts for several thousand human fatalities every year.

▲ King cobras are the longest venomous snakes in the world, reaching 15 ft (4.6 m) in length.

Rapid elapids

Elapids are a family of snakes that are widespread, and their bite is often deadly to humans. All venomous snakes have fangs, but most elapids have hollow fangs, through which venom flows when the snake bites its victim. Most elapids are slender-bodied, fast movers—black mambas can slither faster than a human can run. A tiny amount of their venom—the weight of a banknote—is enough to kill 50 people.

Taipan terror

The Taipan, also known as the Fierce Snake, possesses one of the most deadly venoms in the world. It targets the nervous system, paralyzing breathing muscles. The snake devours its victim once it is dead. Taipans live in remote regions of Australia, and target lizards, rats, and other small mammals.

▲ This taipan is ready to strike—one drop of its venom is enough to kill 100 people.

LYSOL

The fangs of a western diamond rattlesnake are covered with a skinlike sheath that pulls back when they are plunged into prey.

Vicious vipers

Vipers have hollow fangs, which, at up to 2 in (5 cm) in length, are much longer than those of elapids. The fangs are hinged, folding away when not in use. Large glands attached to the fangs deliver a venom that attacks the victim's circulatory system, destroying body tissues and muscles. Vipers also have sensory pits on their heads that detect heat given off by prey, allowing them to hunt effectively under the cover of darkness.

ABOUT 600 SNAKE SPECIES ARE VENOMOUS. FEWER THAN ONE THIRD ARE DANGEROUS TO HUMANS.

SQUEEZED TO DEATH

Boas and pythons—constrictors—do not use venom to kill their prey. Instead, they rely on stealth, and their huge size and strength. They can easily kill animals larger than themselves. The secret to their success lies in a constrictor's ability to grip and squeeze. Once it has caught an animal, the snake wraps its muscular coils around it. Each time its victim breathes out, the snake squeezes a little tighter, until the prey finally suffocates.

▼ A python will check each meal's size and shape before working its extending mouth over one end.

PERFECT Predator

Sharks are awesome hunters of the world's oceans. They have evolved over more then 450 million years to become near-perfect predators. This animal's armory includes: a streamlined body packed with fast-acting muscles, powerful jaws full of razor-sharp teeth, enamel-plated skin, and acute senses.

DETECTION DEVICES

Sharks' extraordinary senses help to make them exceptional hunters. The lateral line, which runs along the length of their body, is made up of sensitive pores that detect any movement in the water. Sharks have large eyeballs, which see partially in color, and some species are able to see well in the dark. Around the mouth, sensory cells are focused in pits called ampullae of Lorenzini. These pits sense the electricity emitted by the muscles of animals nearby.

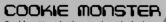

Ampullae of Lorenzini *Nostril* *Eye* *Lateral line*

A shark uses a variety of senses to pick up information about its environment, both near and far.

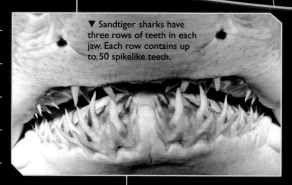

▼ Sandtiger sharks have three rows of teeth in each jaw. Each row contains up to 50 spikelike teeth.

TOOLS FOR THE JOB

A shark's teeth are a guide to its diet. Long, slender, ultrasharp teeth are perfect for gripping slippery squid. Triangular, multi-cusped teeth that look like a saw edge are for carving through flesh and bone. Rows of small, sharp teeth are ideal for grabbing prey from the seabed, and broad, platelike ones can crush the shells of sea turtles.

COOKIE MONSTER

Cookiecutter sharks may be relatively small at just 20 in (50 cm) in length, but they are one of the most savage shark species. A cookiecutter approaches its prey with stealth and speed, then clamps onto its body with its suckerlike mouth, sinking in its rows of sharp teeth. The shark twists its body, making a circular cut, and tears a golf ball-sized plug of flesh away.

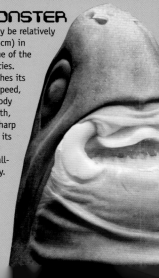

▶ The teeth in a cookiecutter's lower jaw are all joined together and look like the edge of a saw.

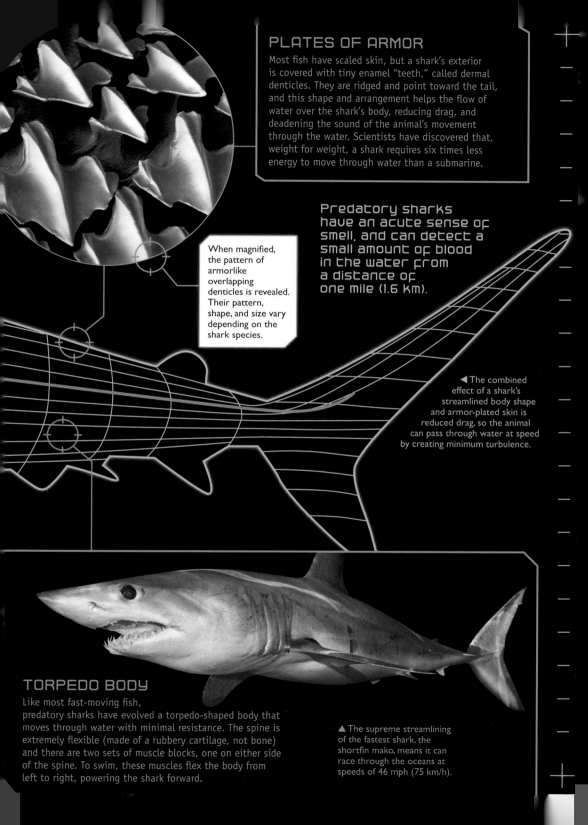

PLATES OF ARMOR

Most fish have scaled skin, but a shark's exterior is covered with tiny enamel "teeth," called dermal denticles. They are ridged and point toward the tail, and this shape and arrangement helps the flow of water over the shark's body, reducing drag, and deadening the sound of the animal's movement through the water. Scientists have discovered that, weight for weight, a shark requires six times less energy to move through water than a submarine.

Predatory sharks have an acute sense of smell, and can detect a small amount of blood in the water from a distance of one mile (1.6 km).

When magnified, the pattern of armorlike overlapping denticles is revealed. Their pattern, shape, and size vary depending on the shark species.

◄ The combined effect of a shark's streamlined body shape and armor-plated skin is reduced drag, so the animal can pass through water at speed by creating minimum turbulence.

TORPEDO BODY

Like most fast-moving fish, predatory sharks have evolved a torpedo-shaped body that moves through water with minimal resistance. The spine is extremely flexible (made of a rubbery cartilage, not bone) and there are two sets of muscle blocks, one on either side of the spine. To swim, these muscles flex the body from left to right, powering the shark forward.

▲ The supreme streamlining of the fastest shark, the shortfin mako, means it can race through the oceans at speeds of 46 mph (75 km/h).

FIGHT-OFF

It is not always easy to predict who will be victorious in a savage encounter in the animal kingdom. Most animals prefer to scare attackers away, rather than engage in a potentially risky fight. However, when opponents do decide to do battle, the winners and losers may come as a surprise.

BUFFALO >>> DRAW DRAW <<< LION

Brawn vs. brain

African buffaloes are equipped with massive horns, tanklike bodies, thick skin, and bad tempers, so a solo lion's chances of success are low. If the buffalo charges, it will swipe at the lion with its horns, potentially disemboweling the predator with a single movement. Although there may be an initial standoff, no lion would risk pursuing this fight. If a pride of lions manages to isolate a very young, old, or sick buffalo, the outcome might be very different.

SNAKE >>> WIN! LOSE <<< TOAD

Final stand

Confronted by a snake, a soft-bodied toad has few choices. They are slow-moving animals so running isn't an option. Instead, the toad puffs itself up with air, significantly increasing its body size, making it appear a more formidable opponent than it really is and too big for a snake to swallow. Some toads add hissing to the display, and have nasty-tasting skin—but none of these strategies will put off a determined predator, and the toad is unlikely to survive.

BEAR >>> DRAW DRAW <<< WOLF

Dead heat

Wolves are pack hunters that employ sophisticated hunting techniques, while bears mostly rely on a diet of roots, fruits, and berries. Wolves and bears do not normally prey on one another, but they are territorial and protective of their young—traits that can lead to deadly standoffs. Both contenders possess speed, brains, power, and massive jaws. However, although the animals will snarl and bare their teeth for intimidation, the confrontation will end in a draw. Combat would prove too costly for either party, and a face-saving withdrawal is the only sensible option.

SPIDER >>> LOSE WIN <<< WASP

Spider snacks

Giant tarantula hawk wasps grow as long as a finger, and have powerful stings 0.25 in (6 mm) long. The wasp attacks its tarantula prey by grabbing one of its legs, and, undeterred by the flurry of irritating hairs that the spider hurls, stings its underside. The wasp drags its paralyzed victim into its burrow and lays an egg in its flesh. The newly hatched larva will feast on the still-living spider.

THE VENOMOUS STING OF A TARANTULA HAWK WASP IS EXCRUCIATING AND CAN CAUSE PERMANENT NERVE DAMAGE IN HUMANS.

ARACHNID Assassins

Arachnids are some of the most successful hunters in the world. Eight nimble legs allow them to leap into action instantly, often seizing their prey before their presence has even been detected. Spiders are arachnids that produce silk—a strong, stretchy thread, perfect for trapping prey—and venom. Fierce-looking scorpions kill with a stabbing stinger.

▼ A net-casting spider holds its web stretched between its legs, ready to snatch any unsuspecting victim below.

Webs, nets, and traps

Orb spiders build typical disk-shaped webs and wait for prey to approach, but net-casting spiders take their web to their prey. Net-casting spiders first spin a small web net. Then, holding it stretched taut between their extra-long front limbs, they leap onto their prey, trapping and wrapping it in silk. Also known as ogre-faced spiders, two of these arachnids' eight eyes are enormous, giving them exceptional night vision.

LETHAL DOSE

Sydney funnelweb spiders combine aggression with powerful venom, making them one of the most dangerous spiders for humans to encounter. They are often found in and around houses and outbuildings in the area around Sydney, Australia. People used to die from the Sydney funnelweb's bite, but since an antivenom was produced in the 1980s, far fewer people have been affected.

◄ The Sydney funnelweb uses its two sharp fangs to strike hard and deliver its potentially lethal dose of venom.

Desert demon

Solifugids may not have stings or venom, but they are fearsome hunters. Their giant fanged, pincerlike mouthparts are the key to their success. These desert-living arachnids usually lurk in cool burrows, or hang from branches during the day. At night, they leave the safety of their dens and go on the rampage, killing large numbers of bugs and spiders, and even larger prey such as rodents and lizards. Their mouthparts can cut through skin and thin bone, dicing a victim's body to pieces in minutes.

◄ A solifugid looks rather like an alien with its bristled face, massive jaws, and beady black eyes.

SOLIFUGIDS DART TOWARD PREY IN THE BLINK OF AN EYE—THEY CAN RUN 20 IN (50 CM) PER SECOND.

▼ A goldenrod crab spider sinks its fangs into an unsuspecting horsefly.

Sting in the tail

The deathstalker scorpion has a reputation as one of the most dangerous on Earth, even though it is only 3–4 in (7–10 cm) in length. Its claws are small and feeble, but this means it is quick to strike with a sting-bearing tail. The venom is extremely powerful, even in small quantities, and quickly paralyzes a potential meal, or an attacker. To a healthy adult human a deathstalker sting is excruciatingly painful, but its consequences can be far more deadly for a child.

Crab soup

Crab spiders don't use webs to catch prey. Instead, they lie in wait, expertly camouflaged in their surroundings, to ambush bugs. Some resemble bark, leaves, or bird droppings, while others are brightly colored to match flower petals. A crab spider's venom is strong enough to kill insects bigger than itself. Once a bug has been disabled by a venomous bite, a crab spider will vomit digestive juices onto the victim, so that its tissues dissolve. Then the spider can consume its victim as a "soup."

◄ A deathstalker's pincerlike pedipalps (claws) are used to grab prey.

ANGRY Birds

Not all birds sit on branches and sing sweetly while eyeing up a juicy berry to eat. Some are born hunters, with weapons to match their savage instincts. Owls and raptors—birds of prey—are notorious, but there are also some unexpected killers in the bird kingdom.

DIVE BOMBER

CLAWED KICKER

Golden eagle
(Aquila chrysaetos)

With a colossal wingspan of up to 7.5 ft (2.3 m) and a top speed of 150 mph (240 km/h), a golden eagle in pursuit of prey is a force to be reckoned with. These raptors dive-bomb their prey, directing a death-blow to the back of the neck. Unlike most raptors, golden eagles often select quarry that are bigger than themselves. The bulk of their diet is made up of small animals such as rabbits and reptiles, but they also attack deer and livestock, including cattle.

Southern cassowary
(Casuarius casuarius)

Cassowaries are large, flightless birds that live in the forests of New Guinea and northeast Australia. They have muscular legs that pack a powerful kick, and, with a 4-in- (10-cm-) long claw on the inside toe of each foot, can inflict a nasty puncture wound. These birds are not hunters, and normally only attack humans to defend themselves or their eggs. They communicate with deep booming calls that are just within the range of human hearing.

Red-backed shrike
(Lanius collurio)

Insect-eating butcherbirds and shrikes have an impressive way to store their food. Once they have caught a small animal or bug, they dispatch it with a vicious peck, and then impale it on a thorn, or barbed wire. This creates a larder that may contain several bugs, small mammals, and reptiles. This gory store of food sustains the birds when they fail to catch anything, and it also impresses potential mates.

BUTCHER BIRD

Secretary bird
(Sagittarius serpentarius)

Long legs help the secretary bird march through the tall grass of the African savanna, stalking prey. These large, slender birds stamp on grass to flush out big insects, small mammals, and snakes to eat. They deliver immense kicks to any animals that bolt, and protect themselves from potentially venomous snake bites by spreading their wings and using them as shields. They can cover more than 19 mi (31 km) in a single day of hunting.

SPEED DEMON

STALKING STAMPER

Ostrich
(Struthio camelus)

Male ostriches usually reserve their aggression for other males, and are swift to attack during the breeding season. They are famous for their bad tempers, so humans and even vehicles are often the focus of ostrich assaults! The tallest, heaviest, and fastest of all birds, the ostrich can reach speeds of more than 43 mph (70 km/h)— and can keep running for an hour or more.

BLOOD
Suckers

Animals that feed on blood have a highly specialized way of life, and are usually parasites. Bloodsuckers have a range of ways to pierce skin to get at the protein-packed, nutritious red liquid. Known as hematophagy, feeding on blood is not confined to mosquitoes and vampire bats—some species of bird, fish, moth, and other bugs also enjoy a bloody feast.

SUPPLY PROBLEMS

A TICK FEEDING ON AN ANIMAL VICTIM

Tick body

Mouthparts pierce skin

Blood vessel

Blood is a wholesome meal, but bloodsucking animals have to be able to find a source, then access it —usually by penetrating scales, feathers, or skin. Techniques for finding a blood source include hearing movement, sensing body heat, following the trail of carbon dioxide breathed out by potential victims, and detecting pheromones (chemicals released by animals). Accessing the blood source normally involves specialized mouthparts that can pierce the host's skin and break into blood vessels, or scrape away at the flesh to create a bleeding wound.

Hungry mothers

Female mosquitoes must feed on the protein and iron found in blood before they can lay eggs. The fly's syringelike mouthpart—a proboscis—pierces skin and delivers anticoagulants as blood is sucked up, to stop clotting. Each mosquito takes a tiny amount of blood, but the damage to the victim lies in the deadly microorganisms that these bugs often leave behind. Mosquitoes can transmit diseases such as malaria, dengue fever, yellow fever, and encephalitis.

▶ Worldwide research continues into the problem of deadly diseases that are transmitted by mosquitoes.

Sucker fish

Sea lampreys are parasitic jawless fish that mostly feed on other fish and marine mammals. They attach to their victims with suckerlike mouths lined with rows of horny teeth that scrape away at the flesh. As they feed, lampreys douse the wound with anticoagulants. Once its stomach is full, the lamprey disengages its mouth from the victim and falls away, leaving a gaping, bleeding wound.

▶ Lampreys become parasites when they are adults, and use their circular, toothed mouths to latch onto fish, such as trout (inset). They feed until they are ready to mate and die after their eggs are laid.

DRACULA BATS

Vampire bats have powerful hind legs and unusually strong thumbs that help them crawl and clamber onto a victim.

Vampires really do exist, but these bats scarcely deserve the gruesome reputation they have acquired since the first stories of Dracula. Most species of vampire bat feed on the blood of cows and horses, not humans. Vampire bats need to consume about two tablespoons of blood a day—more than half of their body weight. They have pit organs on their faces that are covered with heat-detecting molecules to sense body heat. Furtive vampire bats crawl on the ground to approach their prey, and sink their ultrasharp fangs into a spot where blood is close to the surface. They produce a chemical that reduces pain, and keeps the blood flowing as they lap.

TEETH
and Jaws

MAXIMUM ANIMAL BITE FORCES
Figures are estimates, shown in Newtons (N)

Carcharodon megalodon (extinct giant shark)	182,200 N
Tyrannosaurus rex	60,000 N
Great white shark	17,790 N
Saltwater crocodile	16,460 N
Dunkleosteus terrelli (extinct marine fish)	5,000 N
African lion	4,500 N
Hyena	2,000 N
Human	890 N
Tasmanian devil	553 N

About 430 to 445 million years ago the first jawed animals evolved. Their jaws developed from gill arches—the bony parts that support a fish's gill slits. Jaws allowed fish to become hunters rather than just being passive eaters. Today, predators show a range of highly specialized jaws and teeth that can grab, squash, pierce, grind, slice, slash, and mash.

▼ *Dunkleosteus* lived about 360 million years ago.

▼ A lioness in Botswana uses her carnassial teeth to shear flesh from a buffalo carcass.

JAWS OF THE DEEP

The prehistoric seas were home to *Dunkleosteus*, a giant sharklike fish with bizarre structures for biting. Instead of teeth, *Dunkleosteus* had large bony blades in its jaws, which could slice effectively. They were capable of crushing bone—*Dunkleosteus* had the second strongest bite of any fish—and turning fish prey into mincemeat in minutes. This marine monster was protected from attack by an armor-plated skull.

Carnivore club

Meat-eating predators, such as lions, have skulls packed with large muscles and outsize teeth. This allows the jaw to exert a massive bite force with incredible grip. The upper and lower jaw are connected by a hinge joint that allows movement vertically only. Supersized temporalis muscles that operate the jaws are so large that they make up most of the bulk of a lion's head. Carnivore canine teeth are enlarged, sharp, and pointed for piercing flesh, while scissorlike carnassial teeth that line the sides of the jaws shred and shear flesh.

▶ A hyena's teeth are larger than average for its body size, especially the bone-crushing premolars and shearing molars.

Fearless and ferocious

Hyenas are reputed to have the most powerful jaws of any mammal for their body size, and they can crack bone with ease. These strong mammals are aggressive virtually from birth and often hunt in groups. There have been attacks recorded on people camping in hyena territory—campers have awoken to find hyena jaws clamped onto their limbs, taking mouthfuls of flesh in an instant.

Open wide

Hippopotamuses hold a reputation as one of the most dangerous animals in Africa. Despite their exclusively herbivorous diet, these large mammals are extremely aggressive. A hippo's fervent instinct to protect itself, its young, and its territory means an encounter with one may prove fatal. Weighing in at 1.5 tons, with giant pointed tusks that measure 20 in (50 cm) in length, and jaws that can open to nearly 180 degrees, this grass-eater is no gentle giant.

◀ A bull hippo fights other males to protect his mating rights over a harem of up to 30 females.

Double trouble

Moray eels can keep hold of slippery prey thanks to a second set of jaws deep inside their throats. Rows of razor-sharp teeth in the front jaws clench hold of a fish while the rear jaws shoot forward into the mouth. Lined with bigger teeth, these jaws clamp down, and pull the fish down the eel's esophagus and toward its stomach.

▶ Most fish "suck" prey into their throats, but moray eels use their second jaws instead.

Front jaws and teeth

Pharyngeal jaws (rear extendable jaws)

57

PAWS and Claws

Powerful paws and lacerating claws are key weapons, allowing an animal to inflict injury while keeping its own head out of the line of fire. Clawed paws are often specialized, with features that have evolved to match the hunting requirements of their owner.

SPURS OF VENOM

The duck-billed platypus is one of very few types of venomous mammal in the world. Only males possess a curved claw, or spur, on each of their hind legs. These spurs are attached to glands that release venom. Males only use their spurs when kicking out at their natural enemies and other males, especially at mating time.

▲ A platypus's venom is not deadly to humans, but it is said to cause intense pain.

◄ A polar bear's huge paws can be up to 12 in (30 cm) in diameter.

Polar paws

Polar bears are the largest carnivores on land, and they have huge paws to match. In their Arctic habitat, broad paws act like snowshoes, spreading the polar bear's weight on snow and thin ice. They also help the bears to stalk their seal prey—tufts of fur between the toes deaden the noise of their step. Short, stout, curved claws pierce and rip flesh easily, and can haul a seal out of an ice hole to eat.

Indian devils

Wolverines may be no bigger than dogs, but these fearless creatures attack bears and deer, earning them the alternative name of "Indian devil." They are weasel-like mammals that live in northern regions where polar conditions leave predators hungry, desperate, and fearless. A wolverine's paws are large, flat, and furry with broad pads and very long claws. They are perfect for chasing down prey over deep snow, and holding onto a victim while the wolverine delivers a neck-breaking bite with its immensely powerful jaws.

▶ Wolverines both hunt and scavenge, feasting on any animal they can find.

▲ At rest, the hairy frog doesn't look special, but its hidden weapon makes potential attackers think twice.

Snap claws

In the natural world, fact can be stranger than fiction. When threatened, African hairy frogs snap the bones in their feet. The broken bones rip through the skin, jutting out as knifelike extensions on the the frog's fingertips and toes. This gives them an effective set of razor-sharp claws to swipe at an attacker.

CRABS HAVE ONE OF THE GREATEST CLAW FORCES FOR BODY SIZE IN THE ANIMAL KINGDOM.

▲ A coconut crab's strong claws can easily pull its body up a tree to reach the fruit at the top.

Crushing coconuts

When Charles Darwin encountered the world's largest land-living species of crab on the Keeling Islands, he described it as "monstrous." These land-living crustaceans, which are known as robber or coconut crabs, have a legspan of up to 40 in (one meter). Coconut crabs feed mainly on fruit, and their name comes from their ability to open the tough shells of coconuts. Occasionally they use their enormous claws to attack other crabs, and they have been known to turn cannibal and eat their fallen opponent after a fight.

Feline
FIENDS

Cats are famous for their killing skills—their supreme strength and elegance combine to create a sublime predator. Cats all share the same basic body features. They have short muzzles equipped with wide-opening jaws, sharp fangs, and meat-shearing carnassial teeth. They also all have highly developed senses, powerful limbs, and paws that are tooled with retractable claws.

◄ A lioness keeps low to the ground as she stalks prey at dusk.

STEALTH

1

Few animals can stalk their prey with the stealth of a cat. Colored or patterned fur helps a cat to remain hidden in undergrowth as it chooses and follows a potential victim. A characteristic crawl, with its body close to the ground, allows the predator to creep closer—its unblinking eyes fixed and focused on the prey. Leopards move so quietly that they have been known to pluck a sleeping human victim from their bed and escape without a sound—the room's other occupants only find out about the midnight visitor the next morning.

SPEED

2

Felines are able to accelerate fast but, unlike members of the dog family, are unable to sustain a chase for long. Cheetahs are the swiftest of all land animals over short distances. A very narrow body, slender limb bones, almost vertical shoulder blades, and a flexible spine mean this cat is not just streamlined, it can make enormous energy-efficient strides. However, at high speeds the cat gets so hot that it cannot run further than about 1,600 ft (500 m) during a chase before risking death from overheating.

POUNCE

► A caracal's long, strong back legs are perfect for running down speedy prey such as hares and antelopes.

ONE FEARLESS LEOPARD IN INDIA WAS PROBABLY RESPONSIBLE FOR MORE THAN 125 HUMAN DEATHS IN JUST TEN YEARS.

THE FEAR FACTOR

When an animal knows a big cat is nearby, the fear factor takes over. Their body goes into a state of stress, ready to run or defend itself—the "fight or flight" response. Adrenaline courses through the blood vessels, increasing the rate of blood circulation, breathing, metabolism of carbohydrates, and preparing the muscles for exertion. Although felines are superb predators, most of their potential victims escape unharmed.

▲ A gazelle bounds away from its hunter —the big cat.

◄ Mid-chase, a cheetah lowers its head for extra streamlining, and extends its claws for a better grip on the ground.

Leaping and pouncing skills give a feline the advantage of surprise. Prey may have judged their stalker to be at a safe distance, only to be shocked, seconds later, to find a fanged set of jaws looming overhead. Snow leopards hold the record for the longest recorded leap of any cat, at 49 ft (15 m), but caracals and servals are the bounciest cats. Pouncing enables a cat to approach its prey from above, which means it can avoid potential bites and scratches while delivering a lethal blow.

3

In the final stages of a hunt, cats employ speed and strength and go for the throat. With their jaws tightly clamped around the windpipe, a cat effectively suffocates its prey, and the victim usually suffers a quick death. Large cats can hunt prey bigger than themselves, and often drag their victim to a safe location before settling down to eat.

▼ A jaguar clamps its strong jaws onto the skull of an unfortunate caiman.

4

SLAUGHTER

BRUTAL Bugs

▶ A tailless whip scorpion begins to munch through the body of a grasshopper.

You don't have to be big to be brutal. Skulking beneath rocks, lurking in the undergrowth, flitting through the air, and even hiding in our homes there is an almost invisible world of mini-monsters, battling it out for survival.

Acid attack

Giant vinegaroons resemble a cross between a scorpion and a spider, and share some of the most savage characteristics of both. These arachnids—also known as whip scorpions—grab their invertebrate victims with their heavy, armored pedipalps and crush them to death. They deter predators by bombarding them with a noxious spray that is 84 percent acid.

▼ Bulldog ants are only found in Australia. They live in colonies but forage and hunt alone—mostly feeding on smaller carpenter ants.

▼ Capable of killing 40 honeybees in a minute, this giant hornet kills more people in Japan every year than any other animal.

Nonstop stingers

Ants are brutal bugs with vicious stings—they belong to the same family as bees, wasps, and hornets. Bullet ants are named for their stings, which are said to feel like a gunshot, and fire ants hold tight to an attacker and keep stinging for as long as they can. Bulldog ants are fierce, but one look at their menacing jaws should be enough to scare any attacker away.

Big, bold, and bad

In Japan, Asian giant hornets are called sparrow-wasps because at 2 in (5 cm) in length, they look similar to small birds when in flight. Like other members of the bee and wasp family, these insects administer pain-inducing stings, but they also inject a neurotoxin that can prove lethal. Thankfully they usually reserve their aggression for colonies of honeybees rather than people.

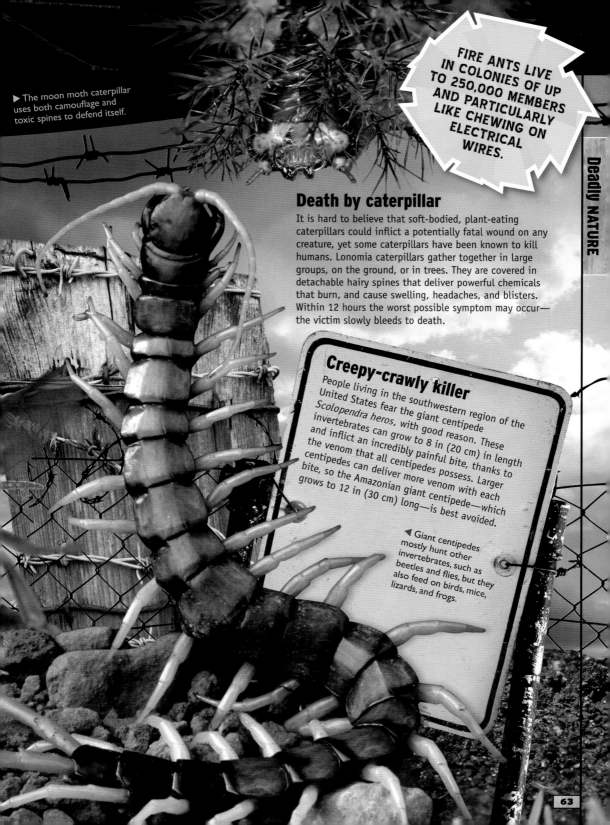

▶ The moon moth caterpillar uses both camouflage and toxic spines to defend itself.

FIRE ANTS LIVE IN COLONIES OF UP TO 250,000 MEMBERS AND PARTICULARLY LIKE CHEWING ON ELECTRICAL WIRES.

Death by caterpillar

It is hard to believe that soft-bodied, plant-eating caterpillars could inflict a potentially fatal wound on any creature, yet some caterpillars have been known to kill humans. Lonomia caterpillars gather together in large groups, on the ground, or in trees. They are covered in detachable hairy spines that deliver powerful chemicals that burn, and cause swelling, headaches, and blisters. Within 12 hours the worst possible symptom may occur— the victim slowly bleeds to death.

Creepy-crawly killer

People living in the southwestern region of the United States fear the giant centipede *Scolopendra heros*, with good reason. These invertebrates can grow to 8 in (20 cm) in length and inflict an incredibly painful bite, thanks to the venom that all centipedes possess. Larger centipedes can deliver more venom with each bite, so the Amazonian giant centipede—which grows to 12 in (30 cm) long—is best avoided.

◀ Giant centipedes mostly hunt other invertebrates, such as beetles and flies, but they also feed on birds, mice, lizards, and frogs.

63

Cold-blooded KILLERS

Most reptiles and amphibians are active hunters. These are ancient groups of animals that have developed a diverse range of hunting techniques. There are cannibalistic "dragons," sit-and-wait predators, stalking crocodilians, slimy salamanders, and even frogs with fangs.

CAUTION: Surinam horned frog

Surinam horned frogs are expert ambushers. Their peculiar flattened appearance allows these large amphibians to partly bury themselves in the ground and remain undetected by prey. When victims approach, the frogs leap into action. Unusually for frogs, they have toothlike bony projections from the jaw, so they immobilize their prey with a single bite before swallowing it whole.

▶ A Surinam horned frog may sit absolutely still for several days, waiting for lunch—such as a bullfrog—to pass by.

DANGER: Nile crocodile

Many savage animals only resort to aggression when provoked, or in self-defense. However, crocodiles almost always attack with a single purpose in mind—getting a meal. Most crocodiles ambush their prey, and typically attack at the water's edge. They lunge forward, take a strong hold with their jaws, and pull the victim underwater. Once there, they will roll around in the water, which can disorientate prey, drown it, and snap its spine.

◀ A crocodile's eyes, ears, and nose are all on top of its head, so that it can lie in wait for prey almost completely submerged.

HE KILLER QUESTION

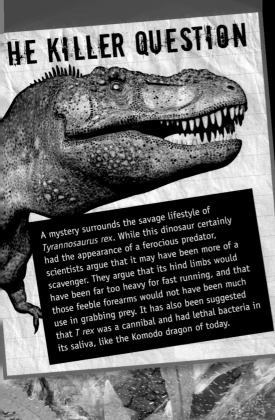

A mystery surrounds the savage lifestyle of *Tyrannosaurus rex*. While this dinosaur certainly had the appearance of a ferocious predator, scientists argue that it may have been more of a scavenger. They argue that its hind limbs would have been far too heavy for fast running, and that those feeble forearms would not have been much use in grabbing prey. It has also been suggested that *T rex* was a cannibal and had lethal bacteria in its saliva, like the Komodo dragon of today.

WARNING: Komodo dragon

The Lesser Sunda Islands in Indonesia are so remote that the existence of their now most famous inhabitants was widely unknown until 100 years ago. Komodo dragons are the largest living lizards, reaching 10 ft (3 m) in length. They combine a monstrous appearance with a savage nature—feeding on almost anything, and attacking large animals, including humans. Adult Komodos will also eat younger members of their own species, so youngsters often have to hide in trees to avoid being eaten.

▼ An antelope's leg disappears down a dragon's gaping throat—an adult Komodo can eat up to 80 percent of its own body weight at one time.

HAZARD: Japanese giant salamander

Salamanders are amphibians, like frogs and toads, but with tails. They are all carnivores, but they can withstand long periods without any food at all. Many are dull-colored for camouflage but fire salamanders have bold yellow markings to warn that they produce a toxic substance. Japanese giant salamanders grow to almost 5 ft (1.5 m). They have slimy, mucus-covered skin and huge mouths. They lie in wait for food to pass by and grab prey with an almighty snap of their jaws.

◄ At night a Japanese giant salamander is alert, but in the day it rests beneath rocks.

RIVER SAFARI

Under the still surface of a lake or the gently rippling waters of a river, undiscovered assassins lurk. Although humans have been using waterways for many thousands of years, the waters still hide many savage secrets. We are only just beginning to understand what an incredible wealth of fascinating animal stories the world's rivers have to tell.

Mystery monster

Giant freshwater stingrays are among the world's biggest river killers. At half the length of a bus, they are strong enough to pull boats along rivers or underwater. Giant stingrays remained undiscovered until the 1990s and new species are now being identified in Indo-Pacific river regions. Stingrays are usually passive fish, but they may attack people who try to handle them. Their tails have arrowlike barbs of up to 15 in (38 cm) that can break through skin and penetrate bone to deliver deadly venom.

▼ Despite their awesome size, giant stingrays are difficult to find, catch, or study.

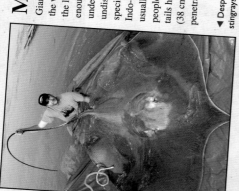

Water bugs have been observed eating baby turtles, and even snakes.

Big, bad bugs

Giant water bugs are the largest insect river monsters in the world. They can walk, fly, and swim, using their wings to store air while they hunt underwater. These huge aquatic insects sit motionless waiting for prey to approach them, then make a grab with pincerlike front legs. Needlelike mouthparts inject saliva into the victim, and its body juices are sucked out.

Man-eating catfish

Tales of man-eating catfish have been around for centuries, and the wels catfish is often named as the number one suspect. These massive fish are certainly equipped to kill, with huge jaws lined with hundreds of small teeth and an aggressive temperament at mating time. While this fish may pose some risk to humans, its natural prey are much smaller—crustaceans, fish, frogs, worms, and ducks.

▲ Little is known about these monster fish, so explorer Zeb Hogan has launched a project to protect them and other freshwater giants.

Survival strategy

The alligator gar is a menacing megafish with a long, toothed snout. It preys on fish, turtles, and birds. The gar's eggs and yolk sacs have a very unusual feature that has doubtless helped these ancient fish to survive—they are toxic to crustaceans and many vertebrates. Crayfish and blue crabs are especially vulnerable to the poison, and even humans are affected just by handling alligator gar eggs.

▶ An alligator gar can grow to 10 ft (3 m) in length and gets its name from its long, toothy snout.

WIGGLING, WRIGGLING WORMS

A primitive beast lurks in the murky waters of swamps in the southeastern states of the U.S.—the alligator snapping turtle. This ancient animal demonstrates an impressive hunting trick—it lies with its jaws wide open to expose a red wriggling structure on its tongue, which looks like a worm. Fish are tempted into the monster's beaklike mouth, which then slams shut.

With its dull colors and strange body shape, an alligator snapping turtle has perfect camouflage.

Wels catfish use their barbels (whiskerlike sense organs) to taste, and feel their way in murky water.

SMASH! BANG! WALLOP!

Gripping jaws, **snipping** teeth, **ripping** claws—for some animals these standard tools of **savagery** are far too predictable. They use rather more surprising techniques to overpower their enemies, and get their point across in style.

Male strawberry poison frogs prefer to wrestle in the mornings. In the afternoon they eat, mate, and look after their young.

CRUNCH!

Two whitetail deer bucks square up for battle. Extra-thick skulls help protect their brains from the damaging effects of a smashing time.

GRAPPLE!

For a male antelope or deer, the rewards for fighting are high and the winner takes it all.

These animals operate harems, which means one male can win mating rights over a whole group of females, ensuring that future generations will carry his genes. In some species of antelope, horns can grow to 5 ft (1.5 m) in length—and particularly impressive horns may help a male to assert his dominance over other males without the need for fighting. However, if a fight-off is necessary, the stakes are high. Broken horns are a common injury following head-butting clashes, but others can be far more life-threatening.

Male strawberry poison frogs are proud homeowners, but they only welcome guests of the female kind. A male spends the morning warning neighboring males to keep their distance, but if one does stray over the invisible boundary a flesh-on-flesh battle will follow. The males hold tight and wrestle to the ground, pushing one another with their strong legs—the loser is forced to the ground and must leave the area in shame.

POISON FROGS HAVE FEW ENEMIES, AS THEIR COLORFUL SKIN IS HIGHLY TOXIC.

PUNCH!

Male Eastern gray kangaroos fight at mating time, but these sparring skills are also useful for battling dingos (wild dogs).

Kangaroos are famous for their kickboxing skills. These marsupial bruisers put everything into a confrontation—jabbing with clawed forepaws, grappling, and delivering mighty kicks from muscular hindlegs.

Hooved animals can use brute force to demolish any opposition. A fast kick delivers bone-crunching force, which is why horses and zebras are animals to be respected. Zebra stallions fight over mating rights and feeding grounds. In the first instance a small kick may be enough to persuade rivals to move, but if that doesn't work a stallion may deliver a series of deadly blows, usually aimed at a rival's head.

THWACK!

It takes great strength and agility for a zebra to launch an attack, but for the victor this vicious battle will be worth the effort.

When males of almost any species square up to each other, there is a show of size and strength. Male swans raise their bodies out of the water, spread their wings and curve their necks—and the smaller bird may turn tail at this point. If not, a vicious battle may follow and can result in death. Wings and beaks are used as weapons.

NIP!

The strongest swan sends its male rival packing with a wallop of the wings and a few sharp nips with a powerful beak.

COOL, CRUEL World

L ife in the extreme habitats of the Arctic and Antarctic poses particular problems for wildlife. Without warmth and light to support much plant growth on land, most of the animals that survive here have to be meat or fish eaters. The outcome of a hunt may spell life or death when the next meal may be many miles, or days, away.

White wanderer

The Arctic fox hunts and scavenges a wide variety of prey depending on its location.

Foxes are among the most successful mammals in the world, and are able to survive in a huge variety of habitats. Arctic foxes exemplify this success because they have impressive adaptations to seasonal extremes in the north. During the summer, their brown coats provide camouflage in woodlands and scrub, but in the winter they grow very thick white pelts, and take shelter in huge underground dens with extensive burrow systems.

A parasitic copepod is just visible, attached to this Greenland shark's eye.

Ice shark

Ancient, slow-moving assassins live beneath the Arctic ice. Greenland sharks are the second-largest carnivorous sharks in the world. They only grow 0.5 in (one centimeter) per year, so a 20 ft (6 m) individual may be centuries old. Young Greenland sharks are likely to prey upon seals. Older individuals often have to scavenge, after parasites attack their eyes, making them blind.

AVIAN THUG

Arctic skuas have a huge range, and spend their summers along northern coasts of America and Europe. They are also known as parasitic jaegers.

Arctic skuas are kleptoparasites (food thieves), predators, and scavengers. One tactic is to threaten other birds until they regurgitate food, which the skua then eats. They attack smaller birds, and even dive-bomb large animals, including humans. Most onslaughts are aerial attacks, but some skuas have been seen sneaking up on nesting colonies of Arctic terns on foot. This approach fools the terns, which did not notice their eggs and chicks being stolen until too late.

ARCTIC ASSASSIN

Polar bears are the biggest and most ruthless of all bears. Their immense bodies are packed with muscles and fat, and they require an energy-rich diet to keep warm, and to power their predatory lifestyles. One bear needs to kill up to 75 seals per year to survive, but can live for up to eight months without feeding. Polar bears are one of the few predators that are known to hunt humans actively for food, although females are most dangerous when they are protecting their cubs.

Polar bear mothers teach their cubs to hunt. These cubs are fighting over whale meat.

KING PENGUINS CAN GO FOR MONTHS BETWEEN MEALS. ONE CHICK SURVIVED FOR FIVE MONTHS WITHOUT EATING.

This king penguin's nasty wound was inflicted by a leopard seal.

Snowy survivor

Penguins only feed in the sea, and can hunt their prey of fish at top speeds of 22 mph (35 km/h), appearing to almost fly through the water. Emperor penguins dive to depths of at least 1,740 ft (530 m) to reach fish, crustaceans, and squid. These birds have sharp-edged, hooked bills and their throats and tongues are coated with backward-pointing spines—features that ensure captured fish are on a oneway route to the stomach. Penguins face predation from seabirds, such as skuas, and leopard seals. One leopard seal may devour 12 Adélie penguins for a single meal.

DEATH SQUAD

There is not only safety in numbers—there is power. When animals work together to hunt and kill, they become a deadly force. Combining efforts means a successful hunt is more likely, and everyone gets a share of the kill. These death squads of the natural world have little to fear from predators or prey.

Lion's share

A pride of lions can dominate the landscape, invoking panic among nearby herds of herbivores. When it is time to feed, the primary hunters—the females—become more furtive. They stalk and surround their prey, constantly checking one another's position, before launching into the attack. Working together they can fell big prey, killing by sinking their teeth into the victim's windpipe, causing suffocation.

TWO LIONESSES WORK TOGETHER TO BACK A WILDEBEEST INTO A CORNER AND PREPARE TO STRIKE.

Canny canids

Many dog species combine superb senses with cooperation, communication, and a strong social structure. African hunting dogs exemplify the canid lifestyle. They live in packs led by a dominant breeding pair, and hunt in groups of six to 20 animals. Their methods are brutal but efficient, pursuing a victim until it almost collapses with exhaustion, and taking opportunistic bites of flesh during the chase.

A PACK OF DOGS TARGETS A LONE WARTHOG, AND THE VICTIM DISAPPEARS ALMOST INSTANTLY IN THE FEEDING FRENZY.

Killer whales

It has recently been discovered that orcas (killer whales) hunt in cooperative groups. These intelligent, adaptable animals will herd fish toward each other and then stun them with blows from their tail flukes. Against seals they employ a strategy known as "wave-hunting." Their ability to learn is key to their success—young orcas watch the hunt, and learn the technique.

WAVE-HUNTING

1. AT FIRST, THE GROUP OF ORCAS RAISE THEIR HEADS OUT OF THE WATER TO LOOK FOR SEALS RESTING ON ICE FLOES.

2. HAVING IDENTIFIED A TARGET, THE ORCAS SWIM AS A GROUP TOWARD AND BENEATH THE FLOE.

3. THIS CREATES A WAVE OR SWELL LARGE ENOUGH TO ROCK OR TIP THE FLOE, CAUSING THE SEAL TO FALL OFF THE ICE AND INTO THE ORCAS' WAITING MOUTHS.

SUPER

POWERS

In the animal world, fantastical creatures and astounding stories of survival and savagery abound. From the murky bottom of the seabed to the dark interior of an insect's nest there are battles to be fought and won—and some of them involve extraordinary powers.

Little pistol shrimps may not look very impressive but these tiny marine crustaceans have a super power that packs a sonic punch. One claw is much bigger than the other—and this is the shrimp's secret weapon. As the claw is snapped shut a jet of water fires out at 60 mph (100 km/h), creating a bubble of superheated air in its wake. The bubble bursts, creating a loud cracking sound and a flash of light. The bang is powerful enough to stun, or even kill, prey.

CRACK!

Pistol Shrimp

A cuckoo wasp is able to infiltrate the nest of a beewolf (another type of wasp), lay its eggs, and escape—all without being detected. It achieves this incredible feat by means of an invisibility "cloak." The cuckoo wasp's skin is coated in chemicals that mimic the beewolf's own skin so closely that the beewolf thinks it is playing host to a member of its own family, not a trespasser. When the cuckoo wasp's eggs hatch, the larvae devour the beewolf's offspring.

SNEAK!

Cuckoo Wasp

BOXER CRAB

KAPOW!

Small boxer crabs employ even tinier friends to help them become more brutal. They hold stinging sea anemones in their pincers and wave them about, like a boxer brandishing his gloved fists. By waving the anemones, the little pugilists show possible attackers that they are armed and ready. In return, the anemones feed on the crab's leftovers.

BOMBARDIER BEETLE

SQUIRT!

An explosive force can be a highly effective weapon, and animals knew this long before Alfred Nobel invented dynamite! Bombardier beetles combine liquids in their bodies to create a hot, toxic, and explosive liquid that they can aim at predators with incredible accuracy. Bombardier beetles are not the only insects to employ explosive defense methods: kamikaze termites and ants spontaneously rupture their bodies to release a toxic flare if their colony is in danger—but at least these bugs go out with a bang!

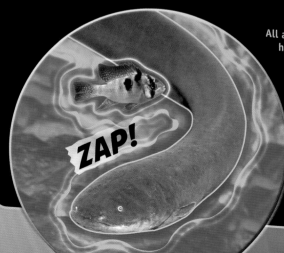

ZAP!

All animals have electricity in their bodies, but few have turned a normal life function into a killing force. Discharging electricity is called electrogenesis and electric eels are masters of the art. Despite their name these animals are not true eels, but a type of long-bodied fish, called a knifefish. Using up to 6,000 special "battery" cells on its abdomen, an electric eel can generate and store 600 volts, which it uses to stun or kill its prey.

ELECTRIC EEL

Wild SCIENCE

Find out about extreme reactions and deadly materials. From highly corrosive acid to explosions inside stars, this is where science goes off with a bang.

◄ A high-speed photograph shows the explosive power of a bullet leaving the muzzle of a gun.

CRAZY Matter

Under normal conditions, such as those that exist on Earth, matter exists in three phases—solid, liquid, and gas. These phases can transform from one to another by changing the temperature and pressure. Matter can also exist in other more exotic phases, but only under the most extreme conditions.

◀ Inside a plasma globe, a high-voltage electrode turns gases into glowing plasma.

See-through solid

Unlike most solids, glass is amorphous—it does not have a crystal structure. With no crystal surfaces to interfere with the passage of light, glass is transparent. Some people believe that solid glass flows very slowly, like a liquid, but this is just a myth. Glass is a true solid because it has a definite shape and volume.

3.6 million °F (2 million °C)

2,700°F (1,500°C)

Pulsing plasma

Plasma, the fourth state of matter, is made of electrically charged atoms and electrons. In nature, plasma is found in extremely high-energy situations such as lightning bolts and stars. Man-made plasmas are used in street lighting and neon signs. Plasma technology can produce bright light from very little electricity.

▲ When glass is melted, it forms a thick, rubbery liquid that can be shaped.

Low-energy gas

Bose-Einstein condensate is a fifth phase of matter named after the two mathematicians who proposed its existence. Scientists prepare a condensate by cooling a dilute gas to within a thousandth of a degree from absolute zero (-459.67°F, -273.15°C). At this very low temperature, the atoms in the gas are at their lowest possible energy state and behave in strange ways.

LIGHT TRAVELING THROUGH A BOSE-EINSTEIN CONDENSATE IS SLOWED TO ABOUT 37 MPH (60 KM/H) AND MAY EVEN STOP ALTOGETHER.

◄ Lasers are used to cool the atoms of gas to make a Bose-Einstein condensate.

Glass container

Laser beam

−459.67°F (−273.15°C)

−296°F (−182°C)

Dry ice

When carbon dioxide gas freezes at -109.3°F (-78.5°C), it is known as "dry ice" because it does not melt into a liquid. Instead, it sublimes—turns from a solid to a gas without going through the liquid phase. Liquid carbon dioxide can only exist under conditions of more than five times normal atmospheric pressure.

-109.3°F (-78.5°C)

▶ Scientists believe that methane clathrate could be used as an energy source in the future.

▲ Dry ice is often used to refrigerate frozen goods for transportation. It freezes quickly and doesn't leave messy liquid behind.

Ice that burns

Methane is a highly flammable gas that solidifies at -296°F (-182°C). However, it can become part of solid water ice at the higher temperatures found in Arctic permafrost or beneath the seabed. Tiny bubbles of methane become trapped between crystals of frozen water to form a substance known as methane clathrate, or fire ice. If you set fire to it, the methane burns while the ice melts.

In the air

We live at the bottom of the atmosphere, surrounded by a mixture of gases called air. As air, these gases are essential to support life. Individually, however, gases such as oxygen and hydrogen reveal a savage and unforgiving nature.

The big H

The first element in the periodic table, hydrogen is the simplest and lightest. Air contains only a tiny amount of hydrogen—0.000055 percent! Hydrogen is lighter than air, so it was used to fill passenger airships in the early 20th century. Unfortunately, hydrogen has another property —it is highly flammable. After several fatal disasters, hydrogen airships were abandoned.

1
H
Hydrogen
1.01

▲ Filled with flammable hydrogen, the Hindenburg airship burst into flames in 1937, killing 36 passengers and crew.

Life-giving oxygen

Oxygen gas makes up 21 percent of air and without it, life would not exist. Living organisms depend on oxygen because it helps the body to convert food into energy. As one of the most reactive elements, it is often found as part of a chemical compound. Its reaction can be gradual—when a layer of oxide slowly forms on the surface of metal. Or it can be extremely rapid and energetic—when an entire building burns ferociously.

Safe or not?

Nitrogen is the most abundant gas in air, making up 78 percent. An inert gas, it does not react easily with other elements. However, in a process called fixation, nitrogen combines with other substances to make compounds including nitrates. These compounds are used by plants to convert energy into food, to help them grow. Scientists discovered how to produce synthetic nitrogen compounds in the 1880s. These are now produced on an industrial scale to make both fertilizer and explosives.

▲ A nitrogen-based explosive, such as TNT, was used to demolish this high-rise building.

Glowing gas

Neon makes up only 0.0018 percent of air. Neon is a noble gas—it does not react with other elements. However, it does react to electricity. When an electrical current is passed through a gas discharge tube containing neon, the noble gas turns into brightly glowing plasma. It is used to make cities fluoresce with colored light.

▲ Neon signs light up New York City, U.S. Neon tubes can be any shape or size and neon gas itself gives off an orange-red light.

Ne
10
Neon
20.18

◄ To extinguish fire, firefighters douse the flames with water to remove the heat, so the fire can no longer burn.

O
8
Oxygen
16.00

Toxic pollutant

A less abundant form of oxygen called ozone forms instead of the usual oxygen. High above Earth, ozone even more reactive than that protects has three oxygen atoms making it two- forms a layer that protects atmosphere, the Sun's harmful ultraviolet rays— in the surface from occurs near the Earth's respiratory as smog— Earth's ozone that attacks the However, when pollutant surface system. it is a harmful

▲ Ozone is one of the toxic ingredients in photochemical smog— formed by air pollution.

N
7
Nitrogen
14.01

ACTIVE Metals

Most of the elements in the periodic table are metals, and many are safe to handle. An aluminum or iron pan, for example, can be heated on the stove or washed in water without a reaction occuring. Other metals, such as sodium and magnesium, react to air, water, and heat with violent chemical fury.

CESIUM IS A PALE-GOLDEN METAL THAT EXPLODES IF IT COMES INTO CONTACT WITH ICE.

GONE IN A FLASH

Francium is an unstable metal that decays so rapidly, it almost doesn't exist. Scientists estimate that there is only about one ounce (28 g) of francium in Earth's crust. Any amount of this metal big enough to be visible immediately vaporizes in the heat produced by its decay. The largest mass of francium that scientists have ever assembled weighed a mere 300 million billionths of an ounce (0.0000000000000000016 g).

▲ When sodium reacts with water, it produces a bright yellow-orange flame.

11
Na
Sodium
23.00

Sodium sizzle

A silver-colored metal, sodium is soft enough to be cut with a table knife. But drop a piece of sodium into water and it reacts furiously, fizzing and dashing around the surface. The exothermic reaction produces heat as well as hydrogen gas. The heat quickly ignites the hydrogen, causing an explosion.

▲ This lump of rock contains a few scattered atoms of francium.

87
Fr
Francium
223.00

Potassium perils

Only small amounts of potassium and water are needed to produce a reaction that gives off enough heat to ignite the hydrogen released. Powdered potassium ignites spontaneously when exposed to air, so it must be stored in mineral oil. If potassium is exposed to air for a long period, its surface becomes coated with a layer of pressure-sensitive superoxide that may explode at the slightest touch.

19
K
Potassium
39.10

▼ A distinctive purple flame indicates the presence of potassium vapor.

12
Mg
Magnesium
24.31

▲ Magnesium burns with an intense white light.

Burning bright

Although magnesium is a highly reactive element, on contact with air, it forms a less-reactive oxide layer. This enables it to be stored and handled with safety. Magnesium ignites very easily. It burns so brightly that it was once used by photographers to provide the "flash" for their cameras.

Dangerous decay

Radium reacts fiercely with water, but that is nothing compared to its other dangers. Discovered by Nobel Prize winner Marie Curie (1867–1934), radium is a heavy, unstable element that slowly decays. This decay produces large amounts of radioactive energy. Long-term exposure leads to diseases such as cancer, tumors, and leukemia.

88
Ra
Radium
226.03

▶ Marie Curie carried out radium experiments without any protection. She later died of aplastic anemia caused by exposure to radioactivity.

▲ Radium generates so much energy that it glows in the dark. It was once used to paint clock faces, making them luminous.

Hazardous
HALOGENS

Dangerous, highly reactive elements are lurking in every room of your home and on every shelf in your local store. No need to panic! The products are completely safe—when used correctly. But if you don't respect the halogens, proceed at your peril...

CHLORINE

Deadly iodine

Iodine is a dark, shiny solid. Minute amounts are essential for a healthy diet and occur naturally in many foods, such as strawberries. When dissolved in alcohol, iodine is used as an antiseptic and disinfectant; it was also used in the manufacture of photographic film. However, large amounts are poisonous and iodine vapor is toxic, causing breathing problems.

▲ Iodine turns from a solid into a poisonous violet-colored gas at room temperature.

53	I
	Iodine
	126.90

Chlorine

Poisonous to all forms of life, green-colored chlorine gas is the only element to have ever been used as a weapon—when it was released onto battlefields during World War I (1914–1918). When breathed in, it reacted with water in the lungs to produce hydrochloric acid, which dissolved lung tissue. However, chlorine's killer nature also works as a lifesaver. Used in disinfectants and at water purification plants, it kills dangerous microorganisms before they can do serious harm.

9	F
	Fluorine
	18.998

Fierce fluorine

Poisonous and dangerously reactive, fluorine gas must be handled with care. It is so unstable that on contact with water, it spontaneously burns with a bright flame. However, fluorine is part of useful products, too. It is one of the main components of refrigerants used in household fridges and freezers. Surprisingly, fluoroplastics—plastics containing fluorine—are some of the most stable man-made substances, widely used for electrical insulation.

199.99

17 Cl
Chlorine
35.45

Bad bromine

Although it is now considered too dangerous to be used in pesticides, bromine is still added to disinfectants for hot tubs and spa pools. Bromine has an unusual property —it interferes with combustion reactions— making it perfect for fire-retardant materials.

▶ Some halogen bulbs contain bromine. They produce brighter light, use less energy, and last longer than normal lightbulbs.

▼ Sodium metal burns and glows when added to chlorine gas.

35 Br
Bromine
79.90

▼ At room temperature, bromine is a dark-brown poisonous liquid that rapidly evaporates into an orange gas.

Tiny amounts of chemicals containing fluorine, known as fluorides, are added to drinking water and toothpaste to make our teeth stronger and more resistant to decay.

LETHAL Liquids

Acids are savage solutions that produce hydrogen ions when dissolved in water, conduct an electrical current, and taste slightly sour. Strong acids are corrosive chemicals, powerful enough to dissolve metal and stone. Weak acids are irritants, causing blisters on contact with skin.

DISSOLVING GLASS

Hydrofluoric acid is highly corrosive and must be stored in plastic containers because it dissolves most materials, including glass and metal. This trait is put to good use, however, as hydrofluoric acid is used to etch words and images onto glass. Extreme caution and care must be taken when using hydrofluoric acid; as well as causing severe burns to exposed skin, it is also deadly poisonous.

RISKY SPILLS

A highly dangerous, colorless liquid, hydrochloric acid is produced by bubbling hydrogen chloride gas through water. A strong acid, it is widely used in the manufacture of plastics and household cleaning agents. Its fumes are irritating to the lungs and contact with the skin causes chemical burns. With more than 20 million tons produced and transported annually, accidental spillages sometimes occur.

Emergency crews require special training and equipment to deal with exposure to acids and other hazardous materials.

DISSOLVING GOLD

Gold became known as the royal metal not only because of its rarity and beauty, but also because it could not be dissolved or tarnished by acid. That is until aqua regia, a mixture of hydrochloric acid and nitric acid, was developed. Aqua regia is used in gold mining to dissolve the metal out of gold-bearing rock. The mixture of acids and dissolved gold is then chemically treated to obtain the pure gold.

Gold in concentrated hydrochloric acid

Gold in concentrated nitric acid

Gold in aqua regia

79	Au
	Gold
	196.97

◄ The brownish tinge in the right-hand tube shows that gold has dissolved in the "royal water."

▼ Karst landscapes, such as the Shillin Stone Forest in Yunnan, China, form naturally from years of carbonic acid exposure.

SHAPING THE LAND

Rainwater absorbs minute amounts of carbon dioxide as it falls through the atmosphere, turning it into weak carbonic acid. Although harmless to plants and animals, the acid passes through small cracks in rocks. Over time, this dissolves the limestone rock, shaping it into peaks and caverns.

Pollution!

When fossil fuels such as coal are burned, they release sulfur dioxide gas into the atmosphere. This gas reacts with water vapor to produce weak sulfuric acid, which falls to Earth as rain. Acid rain is strong enough to kill trees and poison wildlife in lakes and streams.

► Acid rain damages stone statues and buildings.

TOP 10

TOXIC ROCKS

Earth's crust contains many valuable and useful minerals, but some of them can also be extremely harmful to living things—and the dangers are far from obvious. Unlike poisonous animals, toxic minerals do not carry a warning about the dangers they represent.

1 THALLIUM

A soft, silvery metal, thallium is used in the electronics and glass industries. Chemicals containing thallium were once widely used as insecticides and rat poison, but they were banned for being too dangerous. It caused damage to the internal organs and nervous system, as well as death.

81 **Tl**
Thallium
204.38

3 BERYLLIUM

This strong, lightweight metal has a high melting point and is ideal for many industrial applications, such as the manufacture of aircraft and computers. Unfortunately beryllium has major drawbacks—it is rare, expensive, and toxic. It can cause a pneumonialike illness, as well as skin diseases.

4 **Be**
Beryllium
9.01

2 ARSENIC

Arsenic was once used to preserve wood and in agricultural products. But any substance containing arsenic is deadly to all living things, apart from a few unusual bacteria. Short-term contact causes sickness and diarrhea. Long-term exposure causes multiple organ failure and death.

33 **As**
Arsenic
74.92

4 PHOSPHORUS

Phosphorus is essential to life because it adds strength to bones and teeth. But it is far from friendly. Chemicals containing phosphorus are among the deadliest poisons ever made. After a short period, joint pain is experienced. Longer exposure leads to weak bones and kidney damage.

5 CADMIUM

Cd 48 Cadmium 112.41

This highly toxic metal is rare in Earth's crust, but is widely used to make rechargeable batteries because it doesn't easily corrode. If inhaled, it can damage the lungs. If consumed, it irritates the stomach, causing vomiting and diarrhea. Long-term effects include kidney disease and fragile bones.

6 CERUSSITE

P 15 Phosphorus 30.97

This innocent-looking mineral is easily converted into "white lead," a substance that was once used in paints and cosmetics to give them opacity. Unfortunately, lead is extremely poisonous, especially to children, and is now considered too dangerous to be used in household products.

7 ASBESTOS

A naturally occuring mineral, asbestos was once widely used for building insulation because it is incombustible. However, asbestos was outlawed in many countries around the world in the 1980s when it was discovered that inhaling asbestos dust caused deadly lung diseases.

8 SELENIUM

Se 34 Selenium 78.96

The human body needs minute quantities of selenium and it is found in some foods, such as nuts and fish. Larger doses are toxic. Minor symptoms of selenium poisoning include bad breath, fever, and hair loss. Serious effects include nerve damage, organ problems, and even death.

9 CINNABAR

An important ore of mercury, cinnabar is often found near recent volcanic activity. This soft mineral can be ground up to make a rich red-colored pigment called vermillion. It can also be heated to produce the highly toxic element, mercury. Contact can cause shaking, nerve damage, and death.

10 ANTIMONY

Sb 51 Antimony 121.75

This silvery metal is usually found combined with sulfur as kohl—a black substance that is easily crushed to form a slightly greasy powder. The ancient Egyptians used kohl as an eye cosmetic, not realizing that even small doses of this toxic metal can cause headaches and nausea.

SUPER CARBON

ONE ELEMENT CAN TRANSFORM ITSELF INTO DIFFERENT FORMS, EACH WITH UNIQUE AND AMAZING PROPERTIES. IS IT IRON? IS IT CALCIUM? NO, IT'S CARBON! DEPENDING ON HOW THE CARBON ATOMS ARE ARRANGED, IT CAN EXIST AS DIAMOND, THE HARDEST KNOWN SUBSTANCE, OR AS GRAPHITE AND CHARCOAL, WHICH ARE SOFT AND POWDERY.

DIAMOND
20 TIMES HARDER THAN STEEL!

INDESTRUCTIBLE AND SPARKLING

DEEP BENEATH EARTH'S SURFACE, HEAT AND EXTREME PRESSURE TRANSFORM CARBON INTO **DIAMOND**! WITH CARBON ATOMS LOCKED IN AN IMMOVABLE LATTICE, DIAMOND'S TRANSPARENT CRYSTALS ARE HARDER THAN ANY OTHER KNOWN NATURAL SUBSTANCE. BLASTED TO EARTH'S SURFACE BY VOLCANIC EXPLOSIONS, ITS UNIQUE PROPERTIES MAKE DIAMOND THE ULTIMATE ALLOTROPE (FORM) OF CARBON. DIAMOND CAN CUT THROUGH ANYTHING, ONLY MELTS AT A SUPERHOT 6,420°F (3,550°C), REFLECTS ALL FORMS OF LIGHT, BLOCKS ELECTRICITY, AND SURVIVES EXTREME PHYSICAL, CHEMICAL, OR RADIOACTIVE FORCES. PLUS DIAMOND FORMS BEAUTIFUL, GLITTERING GEMSTONES THAT PEOPLE WILL PAY MILLIONS TO GET THEIR HANDS ON!

BUCKYBALL
IMMUNE TO SEVERE IMPACT!

STABLE AND VERSATILE

BURSTING ONTO THE SCENE IN 1985, ALL-ROUNDER BUCKYBALL—FULL NAME, **BUCKMINSTERFULLERENE**—IS THE RESULT OF A SCIENTIFIC EXPERIMENT GONE RIGHT! ITS HOLLOW CAGELIKE STRUCTURE OF 60 CARBON ATOMS ALLOWS IT TO CAPTURE AND CARRY OTHER ATOMS. DEPENDABLE BUCKYBALL WILL NOT REACT WITH ANY CHEMICAL OR DISSOLVE IN WATER. LIGHT AND STRONG, BUCKYBALL IS A HEAT CONDUCTOR, AN ELECTRICAL INSULATOR, AND STOPS LIGHT IN ITS TRACKS.

GRAPHITE
WITHSTANDS EXTREME TEMPERATURES OF SPACE!

THE FUTURE IS STRONGER, HARDER, AND LIGHTER

ONLY ONE ATOM THICK, 300 TIMES STRONGER THAN STEEL, HARDER THEN DIAMOND, TRANSPARENT, SUPERFLEXIBLE, AND AN EXCELLENT CONDUCTOR OF HEAT AND ELECTRICITY... WHAT IS THIS MAN-MADE SUPERMATERIAL? **GRAPHENE**! DISCOVERED IN 2004, ITS CARBON ATOMS ARE ARRANGED IN A FLAT HONEYCOMB STRUCTURE, GIVING IT THE STRONGEST BONDS KNOWN TO SCIENCE.

SLIPPERY AND SOFT

CRUSHED AND HEATED UNDERGROUND, CARBON-RICH ROCKS MUTATE INTO METAMORPHIC ROCK AND **GRAPHITE** IS BORN! ITS CARBON ATOMS FORM SHEETS THAT SLIDE OVER EACH OTHER WITH EASE. THIS SLIPPERY PROPERTY MAKES IT A PERFECT LUBRICANT FOR FREEING SURFACES TRAPPED TOGETHER BY FRICTION. AN INCREDIBLE HEAT SHIELD, GRAPHITE RESISTS SCORCHING TEMPERATURES OF 5,400°F (3,000°C). GRAPHITE IS USED AROUND THE WORLD EVERY DAY—AS THE SOFT "LEAD" IN PENCILS.

COOL Cryogenics

Matter—solids, liquids, and gases—can be heated to millions of degrees, but cannot be cooled below -459.67°F (-273.15°C). This temperature is absolute zero and as substances approach it, they stop acting as they normally do and exhibit strange properties.

▼ Aluminum foil covers *Ariane 5*'s fuel tanks to protect the fuel from external heat build up.

Powerful combination

Inside a typical liquid-propellant rocket, such as *Ariane 5*, liquid oxygen below -297°F (-183°C) and liquid hydrogen below -423°F (-253°C) are kept in separate tanks. At liftoff, they are fed into a reaction chamber where they ignite, producing enormous amounts of heat and thrust to power the rocket into space.

Cold storage

Extreme cold has the same effect on living tissue as extreme heat —it kills, but with an important difference. Heat destroys living structures, whereas cold preserves them. Medical researchers preserve specimens in liquid nitrogen because slow freezing can damage the tissues. Liquid nitrogen reaches temperatures of -320.33°F (-195.74°C) so rapidly that water in the cells cannot form crystals. Some scientists believe that it is possible to preserve entire human bodies. Known as cryonics, more than 100 people have been stored this way, but no one has been revived.

▲ Human cells, such as egg and sperm cells, are stored in liquid nitrogen to preserve them until they are needed.

▼ A soccer player uses a cryogenic cylinder before a game to reduce any swelling caused by injury.

Liquid helium is a vital part of Magnetic Resonance Imaging (MRI) scanners. It cools the superconductive magnets inside, allowing an electric current to flow through them without any resistance. This creates a magnetic field that helps doctors to build accurate and detailed images of inside the human body.

Freezing therapy

Some athletes use low-temperature cryogenic chambers to recover from injury. Wearing nothing but socks, gloves, earmuffs, and a bathing suit—to protect against frostbite—they spend up to three minutes in a small room or container cooled by liquid nitrogen, at temperatures of about -256°F (-160°C). The low temperature causes the body to release endorphins, which speed recovery. It also numbs the body's nerves, providing immediate pain relief and reducing any swelling.

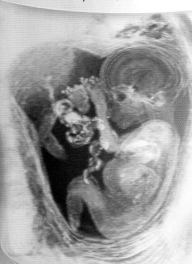

▼ MRI scanners use magnetic fields and radio waves to produce images of soft body tissues, such as a fetus.

WHEN COOLED TO -455°F (-270°C), HELIUM BECOMES A SUPERFLUID THAT FLOWS UPHILL.

CRYOSURGERY

Liquid nitrogen is often used to remove unwanted tissue such as warts, tags, and moles from the skin. Only small amounts are needed because the freezing effect is so rapid, destroying the unwanted tissue in only a few seconds. Known as cryosurgery, this process is much quicker than the traditional surgeon's scalpel and leaves no scarring on the skin.

▲ Tiny amounts of liquid nitrogen are passed through a fine probe onto a wart to freeze and kill it.

Under PRESSURE

Pressure is measured in pascals and normal atmospheric pressure on Earth is about 101 kPa (14.7 psi). We understand the characteristics that substances possess and the way in which they behave at normal pressure. When put under greater pressure, the same substances often behave in sudden and unexpected ways.

Dollar bill on a surface

1 Pa	Gentle breeze
10 Pa	Popping corn
2 kPa	Water boiling at room temperature
2.6 kPa	
101 kPa	Atmospheric pressure for Earth at sea level
350 kPa	Impact of a punch
250 kPa	Air pressure in a car tire
1.1 mPa	An average human bite
30 mPa	

30 mPa
Deep-sea dive
The increased pressure, even during a fairly shallow dive, forces extra gas into a diver's blood. If the diver surfaces too quickly, bubbles of nitrogen may form in the blood. This causes dizziness and a painful and potentially fatal condition known as "the bends." At greater depths, the pressure has a crushing effect on the whole body.

These polystyrene cups were identical until one was taken to a depth of about 9,850 ft (3,000 m). The pressure at this depth—equivalent to 300 atmospheres—compressed the cup to a fraction of its original size.

◀ Water jet cutters are safer for firefighters because they can make holes for the main jet of water without getting too close to the flames.

Chamber pressure of a gun firing

Bottom of the Mariana Trench, 7 mi (11 km) below sea level

70 mPa

110 mPa

690 mPa

2 gPa

Water jet cutter

690 mPa

Under enough pressure, water can cut through concrete, metal, and solid rock. A water jet cutter uses high-speed electric pumps to produce a narrow jet of water driven by pressures up to 690 mPa (100,000 psi)—almost 7,000 times atmospheric pressure. The jet can cut to depths of 18 in (45 cm) and can be as narrow as 0.076 mm—about the width of a human hair.

Meteorite impact

2 gPa

When a 300,000-ton, iron meteorite smashed into Arizona 50,000 years ago, it did more than produce a spectacular crater. The pressure created by the sudden impact was so great, it transformed the minerals in the surrounding rocks.

◀ The crater measures 600 ft (183 m) in depth and 3,900 ft (1,200 m) in diameter.

▼ The liquid metal inside Jupiter can conduct heat and electricity.

Making metallic hydrogen

200 gPa

Scientists believe that the gravity of Jupiter creates so much pressure that hydrogen starts to behave like a metal. To make metallic hydrogen in a laboratory, scientists must achieve pressures of more than 2 million times atmospheric pressure.

1
H
Hydrogen
1.01

The Planck Pressure—only ever reached shortly after the Big Bang or in a black hole

200 gPa   360 gPa   4.6x10¹¹³ Pa

Crude Crackdown

C rude oil is like black gold—a chemical treasure containing hundreds of useful substances. After oil has been extracted from the ground, it is subjected to harsh treatment to obtain the maximum by-products from this precious commodity.

The ingredients

Crude oil comes from the ground. It is formed from the remains of animals and plants. Over millions of years, these remains are covered in layers of mud and rock, creating great heat and pressure. These conditions turn the remains into crude oil, a mixture of hydrocarbons.

FRACTIONING COLUMN

77°F (25°C)

FRACTIONS DECREASE IN DENSITY AND BOILING POINT

CRUDE OIL

FRACTIONS INCREASE IN DENSITY AND BOILING POINT

660°F (350°C)

BURNING OIL

HOME | NEWS | CONTACT

Crude oil is flammable and oil-well fires can occur through human accidents or natural events such as lightning strikes. Due to the enormous fuel supply, the jets of flames are difficult to extinguish. Firefighters detonate explosives to create a shockwave that pushes the burning fuel and oxygen away from the unburned fuel—like blowing out a huge candle!

The breakdown

The mixture is separated by heating the oil inside tall metal towers. This process is called fractional distillation, popularly known as "cracking." Near the top of the tower, the first substances to be released are liquid petroleum gases. Lower down, kerosene and heating oil evaporate and condense for collection. At the bottom of the tower, solids such as wax and asphalt are gathered.

Along with gases such as methane and pentane, BUTANE is mainly used as a fuel for cooking stoves.

BUTANE

Liquid NAPTHA is mainly converted to gasoline, but is also used as an industrial cleaning agent.

GASOLINE for cars and small trucks is by far the most precious product obtained from crude oil.

GASOLINE

Jets are the only engines that can burn KEROSENE efficiently. It is also used in heating stoves.

We rely on DIESEL engines in trains and large trucks to move goods over land.

Engines and other machines require a thin coating of LUBRICATING OIL to keep parts moving smoothly.

LUBRICATING OIL

Ships have special engines that burn FUEL OIL. It is also used for home-heating furnaces.

BITUMEN is used on roads and roofs.

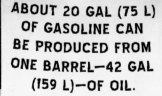
BITUMEN

ABOUT 20 GAL (75 L) OF GASOLINE CAN BE PRODUCED FROM ONE BARREL—42 GAL (159 L)—OF OIL.

Top 10 global oil reserves

COUNTRY	BARRELS (IN BILLIONS)
Venezuela	297
Saudi Arabia	265
Iran	151
Iraq	143
Kuwait	102
United Arab Emirates	98
Russia	79
Libya	47
Kazakhstan	40
Nigeria	37

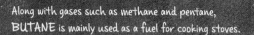

BURNING Issue

Combustion occurs when a substance reacts with oxygen to produce large amounts of heat. Only gases actually burn. Solids and liquids must be heated until they vaporize before they will catch fire. Some substances spontaneously burst into flames, but most fires need an ignition source.

▼ Matches use the heat produced by friction to initiate a reaction between two chemicals—in the match head and on the side of the box. The flame produced ignites the wooden stem.

Invisible danger

Flashovers usually occur in confined spaces when a small fire produces enough heat to vaporize inflammable materials. This creates lighter-than-air gases that become concentrated in the upper part of a room. Even though there are flames below, the gases do not ignite because there isn't enough oxygen. That is, until a window breaks or someone opens a door. The fresh supply of oxygen that enters the room causes flames to flash upward and across the ceiling, instantly turning the whole room into a raging inferno.

▶ Firefighters battle a flashover by directing jets of water at the ceiling.

ON EARTH

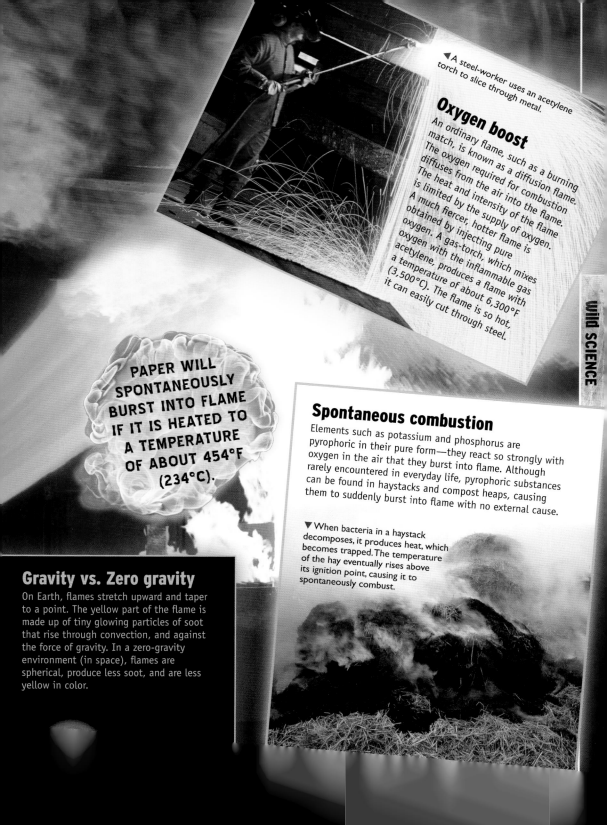

▲A steel-worker uses an acetylene torch to slice through metal.

Oxygen boost

An ordinary flame, such as a burning match, is known as a diffusion flame. The oxygen required for combustion diffuses from the air into the flame. The heat and intensity of the flame is limited by the supply of oxygen. A much fiercer, hotter flame is obtained by injecting pure oxygen. A gas-torch, which mixes oxygen with the inflammable gas acetylene, produces a flame with a temperature of about 6,300°F (3,500°C). The flame is so hot, it can easily cut through steel.

PAPER WILL SPONTANEOUSLY BURST INTO FLAME IF IT IS HEATED TO A TEMPERATURE OF ABOUT 454°F (234°C).

Spontaneous combustion

Elements such as potassium and phosphorus are pyrophoric in their pure form—they react so strongly with oxygen in the air that they burst into flame. Although rarely encountered in everyday life, pyrophoric substances can be found in haystacks and compost heaps, causing them to suddenly burst into flame with no external cause.

▼ When bacteria in a haystack decomposes, it produces heat, which becomes trapped. The temperature of the hay eventually rises above its ignition point, causing it to spontaneously combust.

Gravity vs. Zero gravity

On Earth, flames stretch upward and taper to a point. The yellow part of the flame is made up of tiny glowing particles of soot that rise through convection, and against the force of gravity. In a zero-gravity environment (in space), flames are spherical, produce less soot, and are less yellow in color.

Making a BANG

Bulky and smoky, gunpowder is limited as an explosive. A gunpowder explosion is an example of very rapid combustion, with a speed of up to about 1,300 ft/s (400 m/s). High explosives, which were first developed in the 19th century, do not combust—they detonate, producing a shockwave that travels at speeds of up to 29,550 ft/s (9,000 m/s).

Gaining by graining

To make gunpowder, powdered charcoal, sulfur, and potassium nitrate are mixed with water to form a thick paste, which is then rolled into thin sheets. Before the paste dries, the sheets are cut into tiny fragments called grains. Graining the gunpowder has three advantages. Equal-sized grains are easier to measure accurately. Small grains have a larger surface area, so they burn much faster than a solid lump. Finally, small spaces between the grains in a pile ensure that there is enough air for each grain to burn efficiently.

Magic mixture

The secret of making gunpowder was discovered in China 1,000 years ago when a mixture of charcoal, sulfur, and potassium nitrate proved to have powerful and explosive qualities. The newly discovered gunpowder was soon put to use—packed into bamboo tubes to make simple rockets and bombs.

Rainclouds often formed over battlefields, so people in the 19th century tried to use gunpowder explosions to make it rain during droughts

Rocket launcher

A firework rocket is lifted into the air by a propellant. When the fuse burns into the rocket tube, it ignites the propellant, which launches the rocket upward. When the propellant has burned through, it ignites an explosive charge that scatters colored stars into the sky.

▲ Chrysanthemum fireworks produce stars in a perfect sphere. The brightness increases as it spreads across the sky.

◀ A trained bee sits inside a specially designed cassette.

SNIFFER BEES

Honeybees can be trained to recognize a particular scent, such as gunpowder. Trained bees are placed inside small machines rigged with digital cameras. When the bees detect the odor, they extend their proboscis, or tongue, ready for a food reward. The machine then reports the presence of explosives to a human operator.

Smoke of battle

Gunpowder weapons, such as cannon and muskets, made it almost impossible to see the enemy after the first few minutes of battle. Gunpowder produces thick smoke when it burns—and with hundreds of cannon and thousands of muskets all firing at once, battlefields soon became shrouded in smoke that reduced visibility to a few yards. The 19th-century invention of so-called "smokeless" powder, a type of high explosive, went a long way to solving this problem.

▲ A musket produced clouds of dense smoke with each shot.

Explosive MINDS

Throughout history, scientists have devised methods and formulas to make bigger and better bangs, often making use of ordinary substances such as cotton, sawdust, and air.

BIG BANG

In 1847 Italian chemist Ascanio Sobrero (1812–1888) announced his discovery of nitroglycerine, a high explosive that detonated with devastating results if subject to even the smallest physical shock. It was not safe to handle until years later when it was tamed by Alfred Nobel.

False claim

English scholar Roger Bacon (c. 1214–1294) is sometimes credited with the invention of gunpowder. Although he describes a gunpowder explosion in one of his books and he spread word of its existence, Bacon did not invent it. It is most likely that he learned about gunpowder from the Chinese in Central Asia.

CHRISTIAN SCHOENBEIN

SOFT BUT DEADLY

The first high explosive was made from cotton wool. German-Swiss chemist Christian Schoenbein (1799–1868) treated cotton fibers with nitric acid to produce an explosive that was much more powerful than gunpowder. Although known as guncotton, it was too powerful to be used as a propellant in cannon and firearms.

ROGER BACON

ASCANIO SOBRERO

THE DYNAMITE KID

Swedish chemist and industrialist Alfred Nobel (1833–1896) was a fellow student of Ascanio Sobrero. He became obsessed with making nitroglycerine safer after his brother Emil was killed by an accidental explosion. Nobel discovered that absorbent clay or sawdust enabled nitroglycerine to be formed into small sticks that could be handled and transported without the danger of detonation. This new, safe explosive was named dynamite.

DYNAMITE

DYNAMITE

ALFRED NOBEL

HERMANN SPRENGEL

Kaboom!

Hermann Sprengel (1834–1906) invented "safe" explosives by only mixing the components—highly reactive fuels and substances containing oxygen—immediately before use. In 1885, the U.S. Army Corps of Engineers used 140 tons of this mixture to blow apart rocks at Hell Gate, near New York Harbor—one of the most powerful preatomic explosions.

Trinity tester

The atomic bomb was developed by the top-secret Manhattan Project during World War II (1939–1945). Working under the direction of Robert Oppenheimer (1904–1967), a team of scientists completed the first successful atomic explosion in July 1945, code-named the Trinity test.

Cool explosive

German engineering professor Carl Linde (1842–1934) was a pioneer of industrial refrigeration. In 1895 Linde liquefied air at a temperature of -319°F (-195°C). He then obtained liquid oxygen (LOX) by boiling away the nitrogen. When mixed with charcoal, LOX made a powerful explosive, which was widely used for coal mining until the 1950s.

CARL LINDE

ROBERT OPPENHEIMER

SPEEDING Bullets

When a gun is fired, a propellant inside the bullet burns. This generates gas, which shoots the bullet down the barrel at about 1,000 ft/s (300 m/s). At this speed, the bullet has a lot of momentum and kinetic energy. On impact, the bullet's energy is transferred to its target—with devastating results.

Shotgun blast

A shotgun shell contains up to 500 spherical metal pellets, known as shot. Inside the shell, the shot is held in a plastic cup, separated from the propellant by lightweight wadding. When the gun is fired, expanding gases push the shell along the barrel. At the end of the barrel, the wadding and cup fall away and the shot begins to spread out.

I Wadding and shot leave barrel.

2 Propellant gases billow and disperse.

3 Plastic shot cup falls away.

4 Shot separates from wadding.

SLOW AND STEADY

One early attempt to produce a high-velocity antitank gun involved first slowing down the bullet. The WWII sPzB 41 gun fired a bullet that was larger than the muzzle of the gun. As the bullet traveled along the tapered barrel, it slowed down as it was squeezed to the right size. The expanding gases behind it developed high pressure and the bullet left the barrel with a much higher velocity— up to 4,600 ft/s (1,400 m/s).

▼ The squeeze gun had a range of about 1,600 ft (500 m).

Tank targets

Tank guns fire metal arrows, called penetrators, to pierce the 12-in (30-cm) armor of enemy tanks. The penetrators are enclosed in a lightweight plastic sheath that falls away when the penetrator leaves the muzzle at speeds of about 6,000 ft/s (1,800 m/s).

▲ A soldier loading armor-piercing penetrator ammunition onto a tank.

▶ This bulletproof glass has a layer of plastic between two layers of glass. The plastic makes this glass 100 times stronger than glass alone.

Stopping a bullet

Bulletproofing isn't possible—we can only provide protection against certain types of bullet. Modern body armor uses superstrong plastics such as Kevlar. A Kevlar vest will stop low-velocity handgun bullets. To stop high-velocity rounds, additional protection such as hardened ceramic plates are necessary. Some body armors also use gels that cause the kinetic energy of a bullet to spread out.

SHOCKING Power

Electricity is an invisible force that provides power for much of the world. An electric current is produced as electrons flow through a wire or jump through the air. When we see a spark, it's actually the air being turned into plasma by the power of electricity.

SHOCKING TOUCH

The shock you sometimes feel when you touch metal actually takes place a fraction of a second beforehand. Electricity normally travels through conductors such as metals, but not through insulators such as glass and air. However, electricity can jump between two conductors across a gap of insulating air—the higher the voltage, the greater the distance it can jump.

Caged safety

English scientist Michael Faraday (1791–1867) proved that if you surround yourself with a conducting network, such as a metal cage, electrical discharges will travel along the bars, leaving you unharmed—as long as you don't touch the sides! Faraday cages are used to protect electrical equipment from lightning strikes.

▲ A purple spark of static electricity jumps across the gap between two metal spheres.

▶ Touching the metal sphere of a Van de Graaff generator discharges a small amount of electricity, causing hair to stand on end.

▲ Safely inside a Faraday cage, this lab worker survived a 2 million-volt spark.

▼ Power line maintenance workers rely on strict safety procedures to keep them from harm.

Megavolts

Invented by American electrical engineer Nikola Tesla (1856–1943), a Tesla coil can discharge sparks of million-volt electricity more than 10 ft (3 m) long. The highest voltages, up to 1.5 million volts, are produced at the upper part of the apparatus, which is shaped like a doughnut to maximize its surface area. Once used in radio transmission and to provide high voltages for neon lighting, the Tesla coil has now been replaced by modern electronics.

SHOCKPROOF

Maintenance crews are able to safely work on power lines that carry more than 100,000 volts of electricity. The helicopter that carries workers to a power line must be bonded to the line using a special metal rod. This makes electricity flow around the helicopter. From this point, the helicopter cannot touch anything else otherwise the workers onboard would be instantly electrocuted. The workers are then free to fix the line problems without any immediate danger.

▼ An Australian inventor used a Tesla coil to create this sparkling display around himself.

Hair-raising invention

Invented by American physicist Robert Van de Graaff (1901–1967), a Van de Graaff generator is a simple device for producing high-voltage electricity. Inside the hollow metal sphere, a moving belt causes an electrical charge to build up. When this sphere is touched by a conductor, the electricity is discharged. Large Van de Graaff generators are used to produce the extremely high voltages needed by atom-smashing linear accelerators.

WILD SCIENCE

RADIATION Hazard

When unstable elements decay into other elements, they produce dangerous amounts of radioactivity. There are three types of radiation—alpha, beta, and gamma. Alpha and beta radiation consist of fragments of atoms, called subatomic particles, traveling at high speed. Gamma radiation is the most energetic form of light.

Beta beams

Beta rays are composed of minute specks of matter—electrons, the smallest of all stable particles—traveling at about 90 percent of the speed of light. These electrons, known as beta particles, can damage human tissue. But with little penetrating power, they can be easily blocked by 0.2 in (5 mm) of aluminum.

▶ Beta radiation is used by machines to control the thickness of materials such as plastic. If the plastic becomes too thick, it absorbs more radiation, which is detected by the Geiger counter. This prompts the rollers to move closer together.

Geiger counter

Plastic sheeting

Rollers

Source of beta radiation

Slow and steady

Alpha rays are composed of alpha particles, which are about 8,000 times bigger and heavier than beta particles and travel much more slowly at about 10,000 mi/s (16,000 km/s). Alpha particles are damaging to living tissue, but are so large and slow, they cannot penetrate the skin. They can be stopped by only a sheet of paper.

BETA β

ALPHA α

▲ A detector is worn by people who work with radiation on a daily basis.

▶ The blue light is called Cerenkov radiation. It occurs in water because the charged particles are moving faster than the speed of light in water.

Paper

Customs officers ... gamma-ray ...anners to see the ...apes of cargo ...ide trucks.

Piercing light

Gamma rays travel through matter almost as easily as ordinary light travels through glass—only blocked by lead that is several inches thick. When gamma rays pass through the human body, the high energy they carry causes tremendous damage. High doses cause radiation burns and rapid death; lower doses kill more slowly through cancer and other radiation-induced diseases.

GAMMA γ

LEAD

Nuclear electricity

A nuclear power station harnesses the energy produced by the decay of highly unstable elements, such as plutonium, and uses it to generate electricity. Although alpha, beta, and gamma rays are invisible, the level of radioactivity inside a nuclear power station is enough to make ordinary water glow with a blue light.

DISASTERS

CHERNOBYL, UKRAINE, APRIL 1986

In the evening of April 25, engineers began an experiment to see whether the cooling system could function if the electricity supply were to fail. This caused the reactor to overheat, fuel to explode, and fires to break out. The reactor was not protected by a concrete shell, so radioactive debris escaped into the atmosphere, carried for hundreds of miles by the wind.

▼ Found two years after the disaster, the quince fruit on the right has mutated to a much larger size.

FUKUSHIMA, JAPAN, MARCH 2011

When a tsunami struck the coast of Japan on March 11, it damaged the cooling system at the Fukushima nuclear power station. Without this, the nuclear fuel overheated and caught fire, releasing large amounts of radiation and radioactive material into the atmosphere. The radiation levels were so high that the authorities evacuated the entire area within 12 mi (19 km) of Fukushima.

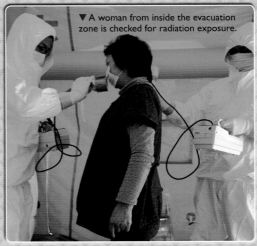

▼ A woman from inside the evacuation zone is checked for radiation exposure.

Star
BIRTH

Stars are made from atoms of the two lightest elements, hydrogen and helium, drawn together by gravity. The actual moments of starbirth are hidden by thick clouds of dust, but nothing can conceal the spectacular surroundings of these explosive events.

① The Eagle nebula

Not-so empty space

The vast reaches of space between the stars are not completely empty. Each cubic inch (16 cu cm) of space contains about 16 atoms—usually hydrogen, sometimes helium, and occasionally another element. These atoms are not evenly spread because they tend to clump together in clouds. The biggest of these clouds are known as Giant Molecular Clouds (GMCs), and this is where many new stars are born.

Compressed gas

When a Giant Molecular Cloud reaches a large enough size, at least 1,000 times the mass of the Sun, it undergoes gravitational collapse—the cloud implodes and breaks up. Vast amounts of energy are released, creating shockwaves that compress and heat the fragments of the cloud to such an extent that nuclear fusion begins. The central region of each fragment becomes the core of a new star.

② Pleiades star cluster

③ Orion nebula

Nebulous evidence

After a Giant Molecular Cloud has collapsed and produced stars, the remains can be seen as a bright nebula in the night sky. The young stars blast radiation into space—creating delicate glowing shapes that will eventually disappear after a few million years.

Scientists estimate that 95 percent of all the stars there will ever be have already been born.

Planetary formation 4

Announcing arrival

Young stars announce their presence by blasting twin, high-speed jets of material out in space. Dust and gas that fall toward the surface of a new star is swirled around and then ejected in long streams above the star's poles. The shockwave from these jets travels at more than 187 mi/s (300 km/s). As it smashes into surrounding gases, it causes them to glow brightly.

New planets

When a new star blazes into existence, its gravity may pull dust and gas into a swirling protoplanetary disc around the star. After many collisions over time, the dust and gas clumps together to form small planetesimals, which eventually combine to form planets. Astronomers have so far discovered more than 1,000 planets that orbit around stars other than the Sun.

Stellar jets 5

6 **Bok globule**

Starry globules

Bok globules—small, dense clouds of dust and gas that block light— were discovered last century by the astronomer Bart Bok (1906–1983). Astronomers believe that new stars can be formed inside Bok globules when dust and gas contract under the gravity of the clouds.

Tough MACHINES

Meet the movers and shakers—these heavy-duty machines are built to go the distance, operating in some of the harshest conditions imaginable.

◄ A group of engineers are dwarfed by the gigantic bucket-wheel excavator that they are operating at an opencast mine.

Tough MACHINES

HAULING
Power

The toughest transport jobs are carried out by machines able to carry the biggest and heaviest loads. At sea, heavy-lift ships ferry colossal cargoes. On land, Herculean mining trucks haul heavy ore, while rugged transporters with dozens of wheels move awkward and outsize loads. In the air, gravity-defying cargo planes can transport enormous payloads weighing up to 550,000 lb (250 tons).

◄ An enormous ALMA transporter hauls a 253,000-lb (115-ton) radio telescope up a mountain in Chile's Atacama Desert.

A COLOSSAL 28-WHEELER
Two specially built transporters are being used to move 50 radio telescopes to a new space observatory on a high plateau in Chile. Named Otto and Lore, each 387,000-lb (130-ton) vehicle has 28 wheels to spread its heavy load and two mighty engines to power it the 17 mi (27 km) to the observatory.

Mining monsters
Vast quantities of ore are brought out of mines to be processed into metals. The biggest trucks in the world are used for this work. Fully loaded, they can weigh the same as 400 family cars. Each of their tires stands about 11 ft (3.5 m) tall and costs $42,500 (£27,500).

LAND

CATERPILLAR 797F
MAXIMUM LOAD:
800,000 LB (363 TONS)

▲ The Caterpillar 797F has a 4,000-hp engine, which powers it along at a top speed of 42 mph (68 km/h) fully loaded.

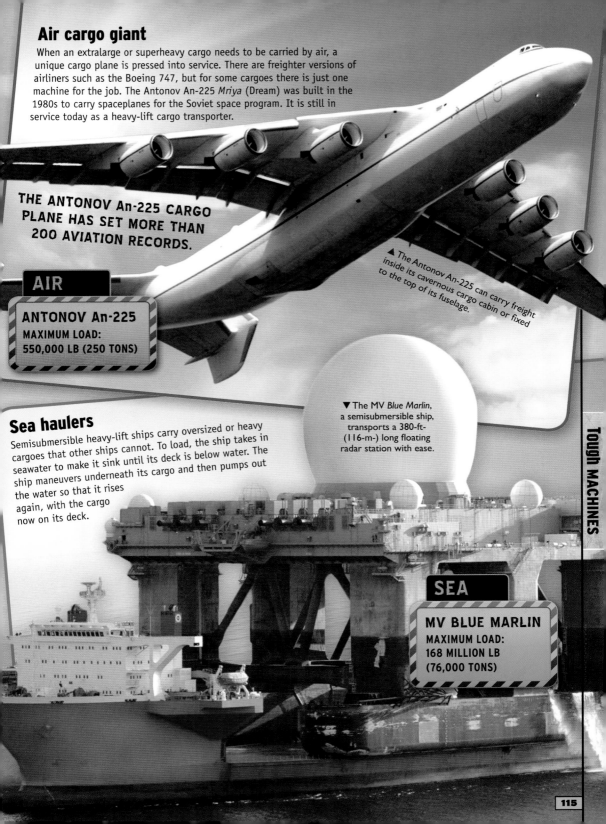

Air cargo giant

When an extralarge or superheavy cargo needs to be carried by air, a unique cargo plane is pressed into service. There are freighter versions of airliners such as the Boeing 747, but for some cargoes there is just one machine for the job. The Antonov An-225 *Mriya* (Dream) was built in the 1980s to carry spaceplanes for the Soviet space program. It is still in service today as a heavy-lift cargo transporter.

THE ANTONOV An-225 CARGO PLANE HAS SET MORE THAN 200 AVIATION RECORDS.

▶ The Antonov An-225 can carry freight inside its cavernous cargo cabin or fixed to the top of its fuselage.

AIR

ANTONOV An-225
MAXIMUM LOAD:
550,000 LB (250 TONS)

Sea haulers

Semisubmersible heavy-lift ships carry oversized or heavy cargoes that other ships cannot. To load, the ship takes in seawater to make it sink until its deck is below water. The ship maneuvers underneath its cargo and then pumps out the water so that it rises again, with the cargo now on its deck.

▼ The MV *Blue Marlin*, a semisubmersible ship, transports a 380-ft- (116-m-) long floating radar station with ease.

SEA

MV BLUE MARLIN
MAXIMUM LOAD:
168 MILLION LB
(76,000 TONS)

EARTH Movers

The biggest digging machines do one of the most formidable jobs there is. In mines and quarries, their enormous metal buckets tear into the ground, gouging out vast amounts of metal ore, coal, and earth. These giant diggers are aided by earth-moving machines such as bulldozers and loaders.

▶ In surface mines, bucket-wheel excavators strip away the earth and rock lying on top of coal. This one works in the Nochten open-pit mine in Germany.

Bucket beast

Giant bucket-wheel excavators are the biggest land machines ever made. They have a large rotating wheel attached to a long, counterweighted boom, which is pushed into the ground. As the wheel turns, buckets around its rim scoop up rock and earth. The biggest bucket-wheel excavator, Bagger 293, is 740 ft (225 m) long, 315 ft (96 m) tall, and its bucket wheel is more than 70 ft (21 m) across.

▶ Walking diggers are used to excavate on the roughest, steepest terrain, where most excavators cannot go.

WALKING DIGGERS

Excavators usually run on tracks to spread their weight over a bigger area and stop them from sinking into soft ground. The Menzi Muck A91 excavator is different— it can walk! The driver can move each of the wheels independently to make the excavator walk up steep slopes and over boulders. Spiked feet extend out from the wheel arms, into the ground, for better stability.

Mega loaders

Mining trucks have to be loaded quickly—they cost millions to buy and run, so time spent standing idle is expensive. Giant loaders are designed specially to fill these mega trucks. A large loader's bucket can scoop up tons of material, and raise it up more than 20 ft (6 m) in the air. This allows the loader to deposit the load in the center of the truck, keeping it balanced.

Oil-powered muscle

The most widely used digging machines are hydraulic excavators, but only the supersized variants of these work in the mining industry. Equipped with a cavernous bucket up to 18.5 ft (5.5 m) wide, attached to a mechanical arm, a hydraulic excavator digs, lifts, and loads rock and earth. The high-pressured oil in the hydraulic system is controlled by the driver, and generates energy to move the arm and bucket.

▲ A gigantic hydraulic power shovel can excavate almost 200,000 lb (90 tons) of rock with every scoop.

THE BIGGEST BUCKET-WHEEL EXCAVATOR CAN DIG ENOUGH EARTH IN A DAY TO FILL 96 OLYMPIC-SIZED SWIMMING POOLS.

▼ A huge engine provides the power a loader needs. The largest loaders have engines the size of a small family car.

Super dozers

Bulldozers are tough earth-moving machines. The biggest kind, Komatsu D575, is known as a super dozer. It has a 12-ft- (3.5-m-) long blade, which weighs around 22,400 lb (10 tons). Powered by a 1,150-hp engine, the dozer can push more than 330,000 lb (150 tons) of earth—the same weight as 30 elephants. If the ground is hard, a clawlike ripper at the rear of the dozer is lowered to break it up.

▲ This Komatsu D575 super dozer is as powerful as a supercar but about 90 times heavier.

SHAPING
the Seabed

The shape of the seabed sometimes has to be altered, usually to deepen waterways for shipping. Ships called dredges, equipped with scoops, cutters, and suckers, carry out this underwater excavation. Dredges also mine sand and gravel from the seabed to supply the construction industry, or pump it onto the shore to restore eroded beaches and create new land.

Chain of buckets

The bucket dredge is a heavy-duty digging machine that can work from the shore or be mounted on a ship. The buckets are fixed to a continuous chain, like a huge bicycle chain, which is circulated by a motor. Beneath the water, the buckets scrape the seabed, scooping up mud, then empty the material into a chute as they are tipped upside down.

◄ Bucket chain dredges are used for clearing shallow waterways. The biggest can scoop up 500,000 cu ft (14,150 cu m) of mud per hour.

► A dredge sucks up and pumps out sand from the seabed. This is called "rainbowing."

Heavy metal spuds anchor the ship in position

▲ The biggest cutter suction dredges can reshape the seabed in water more than 100 ft (30 m) deep.

Spraying sand

A dredge can store the sand it excavates from the seabed in tanks inside the ship. When the tanks have to be emptied, the sand can be sent ashore through an underwater pipeline, but it's easier and less expensive to siphon it straight out of the ship. Powerful pumps on the ship can spray the sand onto a beach to build up the sand level, or to create a new artificial island.

A frame called a "ladder" supports the suction tube

Cutter suckers

For large-scale operations where the seafloor is hard, cutter suction dredges are used. This kind of ship is equipped with a rotating cutter head at the end of its suction tube. Before dredging, the ship drops metal poles called spuds into the seabed to anchor it. Then, as the ship moves from side to side, the cutter carves the rocky bed into small pieces, which are sucked up to the ship for disposal.

A clamshell dredge bucket is raised from the seabed full of silt.

ABOUT ONE FIFTH OF THE NETHERLANDS IS MADE OF EARTH DREDGED FROM THE SEABED.

Scooping mud

Grab dredges are used to excavate in shallow water. The grab, usually a two-piece, hinged bucket called a clamshell, is suspended on a wire from a crane that is fixed to a ship. It is lowered in the "open" position to the seabed, then closed to bite into the sediment.

The suction tube sucks up the loosened material

MAKING ISLANDS

A series of artificial islands have been built off the coast of Dubai by dredging. Ten of the world's biggest dredges vacuumed sand from the bottom of the Persian Gulf and piled it up to create the islands. Each ship filled its onboard tanks in less than an hour and then pumped the sand out fast enough to fill an Olympic-sized swimming pool in four minutes.

▶ The Palm Jumeirah island was created from 3.5 billion cu ft (100 million cu m) of rock and sand dredged from the bottom of the Persian Gulf.

The cutting head grinds up rock

WEIGHT Lifters

When it comes to heavy lifts, cranes are crucial. The building of massive ships, towering skyscrapers, and enormous oil platforms relies on hefty loads being hoisted into position. These powerful lifters come in many forms—from tall, slim tower cranes used on construction sites to floating cranes that shift impressive weights at sea.

Taisun lifts part of a drilling vessel, weighing an awesome 42 million lb (19,000 tons).

Shipyard heavyweight

Taisun is the world's largest crane and is in use at the Yantai Raffles Shipyard in China, where it lifts parts of ships and drilling rigs into position. It can handle more weight in a single lift than any other crane in the world—up to 50 million lb (22,700 tons).

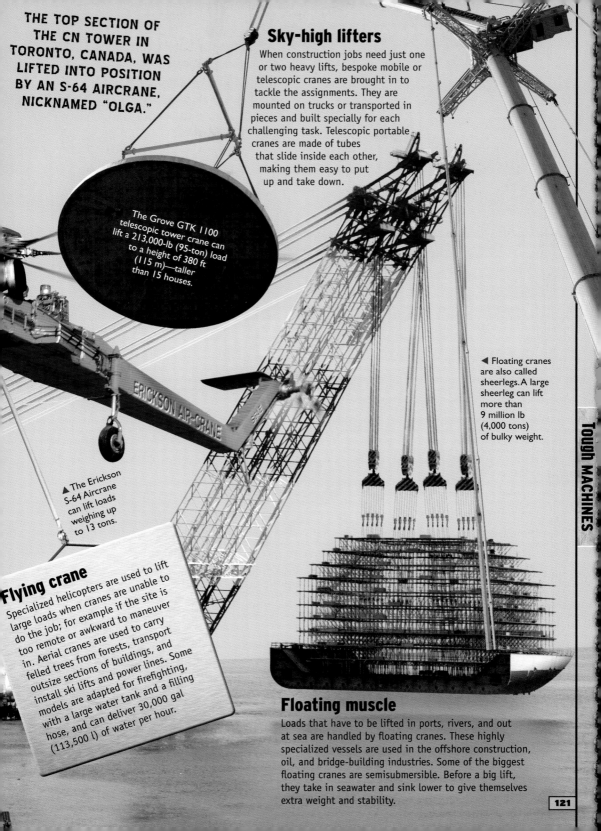

THE TOP SECTION OF THE CN TOWER IN TORONTO, CANADA, WAS LIFTED INTO POSITION BY AN S-64 AIRCRANE, NICKNAMED "OLGA."

Sky-high lifters

When construction jobs need just one or two heavy lifts, bespoke mobile or telescopic cranes are brought in to tackle the assignments. They are mounted on trucks or transported in pieces and built specially for each challenging task. Telescopic portable cranes are made of tubes that slide inside each other, making them easy to put up and take down.

The Grove GTK 1100 telescopic tower crane can lift a 213,000-lb (95-ton) load to a height of 380 ft (115 m)—taller than 15 houses.

◄ Floating cranes are also called sheerlegs. A large sheerleg can lift more than 9 million lb (4,000 tons) of bulky weight.

▲ The Erickson S-64 Aircrane can lift loads weighing up to 13 tons.

Flying crane

Specialized helicopters are used to lift large loads when cranes are unable to do the job; for example if the site is too remote or awkward to maneuver in. Aerial cranes are used to carry felled trees from forests, transport outsize sections of buildings, and install ski lifts and power lines. Some models are adapted for firefighting, with a large water tank and a filling hose, and can deliver 30,000 gal (113,500 l) of water per hour.

Floating muscle

Loads that have to be lifted in ports, rivers, and out at sea are handled by floating cranes. These highly specialized vessels are used in the offshore construction, oil, and bridge-building industries. Some of the biggest floating cranes are semisubmersible. Before a big lift, they take in seawater and sink lower to give themselves extra weight and stability.

SMASH and DESTROY

Big buildings are constructed to last, so demolishing them is a difficult task. Sometimes explosives are used to blow them up, but more often buildings have to be taken down piece by piece. Only machines that can punch through concrete, slice through steel, and endure falling rubble are tough enough for the job.

Demolition diggers

Excavators are designed for digging, but they can be used for destruction, too. Using its strong mechanical arm and bucket, an excavator can tear down walls and ceilings. The bucket can also be replaced with more specialized tools for hammering, cutting, and smashing its way through metal and concrete.

Pulverizer
Jaws with rows of metal teeth bite through concrete, reducing it to rubble.

Hammer
Smashes up large blocks on the ground for easy transportation.

Heavy-duty destroyers

Demolition is tough, hazardous work, so excavators intended for this task are modified to be extrastrong and supertough. The cab windows are covered with metal grilles to shield against falling rubble. Heavy-duty, double-thickness doors reduce side-impact damage. Underneath, thick metal plating protects the vehicle from being damaged by jagged metal and other sharp debris on the ground. The cab may also be sound-dampened to prevent the operator suffering hearing damage.

MORE THAN 200 BUILDINGS WERE DEMOLISHED TO CLEAR LAND FOR THE 2012 OLYMPIC GAMES IN LONDON.

Grapple
Gripping jaws handle and sort loose material and irregular-shaped loads.

High-reach arm
Fitted with any attachment, a high-reach excavator's extralong arm can dismantle a building's upper floors.

Bucket
Edged with teeth, the bucket can push or pull down walls and move loads of heavy rubble for disposal.

Reach for the sky

The high-reach excavator has an extralong boom arm, designed to reach the parts of buildings that standard excavators cannot. Their longer arms, which are usually about 100 ft (30 m) in length, can stretch to the upper floors of a building and take it to pieces. Much longer arms are also available—up to 300 ft (90 m) in length.

SWINGING WRECKER

First used in the 19th century, the brutal wrecking ball is the traditional demolition tool. A heavy steel sphere weighing up to 6 tons was suspended from a crane and dropped or swung against a building to smash down its walls. Although simple and effective, this method is imprecise, and the ball difficult to control. Today, safer and more efficient methods, such as controlled blasting charges, have taken over.

▶ A wrecking ball's weight and brute force smashes a building to bits.

DRILLING Force

Oil and gas production, mining, and major construction projects all involve drilling deep holes in the ground. Huge, supertough drills grind through thousands of feet of rock to reach oil and gas, and in mines they bore holes for explosives that blast valuable ore out of the earth. At the poles, specialized drills extract deep ice cores that hold precious information about Earth's climate.

▼ The largest augers can drill holes up to 10 ft (3 m) in diameter and more than 160 ft (50 m) deep.

Piles of drilling

Before a building's foundations are laid, an auger may be needed to bore holes. This supersized tool has a helix-shaped screwing blade, which carries the drilled earth upward as it drives deeper into the ground. The auger leaves a neat, deep hole, which is filled with liquid concrete and a steel reinforcing cage. This process is repeated to form a set of strong underground legs called piles.

Priceless ice cores

Scientists use drills to obtain crucial information held in the deep Antarctic ice. An ice core drill is more than 30 ft (10 m) long. It has a hollow, metal barrel attached to one end, or core, as it collects the ice sample, or core, as it bores down. Each time the drill is lowered, it can retrieve a core up to 20 ft (6 m) long. Many cores are extracted from the same hole, down to a depth of 10,000 ft (3,000 m) or more. The deepest ice core can tell us about the environment and climate more than 100,000 years ago.

THE TOUGHEST OIL WELL DRILL BITS ARE ENCRUSTED WITH DIAMONDS, MAKING THEM 50 TIMES STRONGER THAN STEEL.

This hollow drill has an ice core inside it. The core will be pushed out and packed in plastic to keep it clean.

Wells of oil

Drilling through solid rock to reach oil and gas requires a tough drilling machine. The end that cuts through the rock is called the drill bit. There are different types of bit depending on the hardness of the rock that's being drilled through. The most common type is the rotary bit. As it rotates, hard teeth grind the rock away.

DRILLING AN OIL WELL

Whether on land or at sea, oil rigs use the same drilling technique. The drill pipe with a cutting bit on the end hangs from a tower called a derrick. A motor rotates the pipe and the cutting bit bores into the ground. As the drill goes deeper, more sections of pipe are added until the drill reaches the required depth. Offshore drilling rigs in shallow water stand on the seabed, but deep-water drilling rigs use floating platforms.

▶ Typically, oil wells are about 5,000 ft (1,500 m) deep. However, some rigs can drill down to a depth of 40,000 ft (12,200 m).

Derrick

Rotary drive

Mud pump

Engines

Casing

Drill pipe

Drill bit

▼ The operator of this rock drilling jumbo steers two rock drills mounted on arms.

Drill bit

▲ A rotary drill is lowered into an oil well. The drill is tipped with grinding teeth.

Jumbo drillers

Machines called drilling jumbos are used underground to extend mines and tunnels. A drilling jumbo has up to three computer-controlled robot arms, which each hold a drilling head precisely in position to bore into the solid rock simultaneously. The tough drills tear through 3–6 ft (1–2 m) of rock per minute. The bored holes are then packed with explosives and blasted to extend the mine or tunnel.

COLOSSAL Tunnelers

Some of the world's longest road and rail tunnels are dug by massive machines called tunnel boring machines (TBMs). The biggest TBMs weigh several thousand tons and are as long as four soccer fields. They move along underground like huge mechanical earthworms, carving tunnels out of the rock.

▶ A tunneler scrambles across excavated rock in front of a TBM cutter head under the Alps.

Grinding rock

A TBM works by pushing a cutter head—a rotating cutting disk—against the rock in front of it. As the cutter head spins slowly, its teeth grind away the rock. Conveyors carry the rock, or spoil, back through the machine, to rail wagons that take it to the surface. The machine can cut through 6 ft (2 m) of rock an hour.

Spoil conveyor belt
Carries waste material away

Cutter head
Up to 49 ft (15 m) in diameter

Concrete tunnel lining

Gripper shoes

Cockpit
TBM is controlled from here

▲ To advance, a TBM's gripper shoes lock into the rock walls and push the machine forward.

Hydraulic motors

Strong-arm tactics

A tunnel needs a strong lining to stop the weight of the ground above it from caving in. The lining is usually made of huge, heavy concrete blocks. Each block, or segment, can weigh several tons. A TBM has a powerful mechanical arm to pick up each segment and lift it into position against the tunnel wall.

▼ A worker checks the fit of the concrete blocks lining the Channel Tunnel between England and France.

STAYING ON COURSE

Steering a tunnel boring machine is tricky when you're underground surrounded by rock. One guidance system uses a laser to keep the machine on course. A pencil-thin beam of light from the laser is aimed down the tunnel to a target on the machine. The machine is steered left, right, up, or down to keep the light in the middle of the target.

▼ A red laser beam shines down a tunnel to guide a TBM on exactly the right path.

▶ A roadheader's cutter is covered with dozens of tough teeth called picks.

Custom cutters

Tunnels that are too short or awkwardly shaped for a tunnel boring machine are made by using explosives or a machine called a roadheader. It has a mechanical arm with a drum on the end that is covered with metal teeth. As the drum spins, the operator steers the arm to carve out any shape of tunnel or cavern.

ARMOR PLATE

Military vehicles have to work in some of the most difficult and dangerous conditions imaginable, often while under attack. Many are armored with thick metal plates to protect the crews inside. As well as protection, this also adds weight—a heavily armored tank can weigh up to 70 tons.

ARMORED BRIDGE LAUNCHER

ONLY $200,000

Got a river to cross? You need a bridge launcher.

The British Titan model is built on a Challenger 2 tank chassis, so you know it's up to the job. It's probably the fastest and best-protected bridge launcher in the world. Within two minutes, the bridge is unloaded and laid by powerful computer-controlled hydraulic rams, without the crew even having to leave the vehicle!

VITAL STATS

Name: Titan Armored Vehicle Bridge Launcher
Manufacturer: BAE Systems
Top speed: 37 mph (59 km/h)
Weight: 69 tons
Engine: 1,200-hp Perkins CV12 diesel
Armament: 7.62-mm machine gun and space to carry man-portable antitank weapons
Crew: 3

MIGHTY MASTIFF

Troops to transport? Convoys to protect? The Mastiff is the ideal set of wheels for the job.

This six-wheeled powerhouse, based on the U.S. Army's Cougar armored vehicle, has proved itself in service with the British Army. Its heavy armor and shock-mounted seats give great blast protection and a thermal imager lets you drive it at night without lights.

This example is nearly new with only one previous owner—the British Army.

ONLY $400,000

VITAL STATS

Name: Mastiff Protected Patrol Vehicle
Manufacturer: Force Protection Industries (modified for the British Army by NP Aerospace)
Top speed: 55 mph (88 km/h)
Weight: 30 tons
Engine: 330-hp Caterpillar C-7 diesel
Armament: 7.62-mm general purpose machine gun, 12.7-mm heavy machine gun, or 40-mm automatic grenade launcher
Crew: 2 plus 8 passengers

ONLY MILLION

TAL STATS
ne: Abrams M1A2 SEP
n battle tank
nufacturer:
neral Dynamics
speed:
mph (68 km/h)
ight: 69.5 tons
ine: 1,500-hp turbine
in armament:
-in (119-mm) gun
ew: 4 (commander,
ver, gunner, and loader)

PHENOMENAL FIREPOWER

This is your chance to own the best.
The Abrams is the main battle tank operated by the U.S. Army and Marine Corps, and has unrivaled armor protection.
With all the firepower you'll ever need, the lethal 4.7-in (119-mm) main gun is guided by a laser rangefinder and computer-controlled targeting system. As well as ground targets, it can fire at low-flying aircraft. With excellent maneuverability and speed, it's the ultimate offroad vehicle.

DIG THIS!
THE ALL-NEW ARMORED LIMO

Not all armored vehicles are in military service. Leading politicians and businessmen often travel in cars that have been fitted with armor plates and bulletproof glass. Cash is transported between banks and businesses in armored security vehicles, and most police forces have some armored cars in their fleet.

RMORED AMPHIBIAN

Assault Amphibious Vehicle for sale—great condition, low mileage, and one careful owner—the Marine Corps.
Travel on land or in water, and take up to 25 friends with you—there's plenty of room in the back. An aluminum hull makes it light and fast, but its armor is tough enough to withstand any amount of small arms fire.

ONLY $150,000

VITAL STATS
Name: AAV7A1 Assault Amphibious Vehicle
Manufacturer: BAE Systems
Top speed: 45 mph (72 km/h) on land,
8 mph (13 km/h) in water
Weight: 32 tons
Engine: 400-hp Cummins VT400 diesel
Armament: Mk19 grenade launcher,
M2HB machine gun
Crew: 3 plus 25 passengers or 10,000 lb
(4.5 tons) of cargo

TOUGH RESCUERS

If you're trapped on a sinking boat or in a burning building, you need help—fast! Luckily, all sorts of emergency vehicles and rescuers are ready to come to your aid. Fire trucks are equipped to deal with many emergencies, not just fires. There are also highly specialized rescue vehicles for dealing with aircraft fires and submarines trapped underwater.

▶ A rescue helicopter carrying doctors lands on a mountaintop to help injured climbers.

1 Air-sea rescue

From a mountainside accident to someone in trouble at sea, versatile rescue helicopters deal with a range of search and rescue emergencies. They can maneuver with extreme precision, hover in position, fly through tight spaces, and land and take off again in seconds. If there isn't a safe place to land, a helicopter can winch people up, and rush them to hospital if necessary.

2 High-level firefighting

When firefighters tackle a blaze high above ground level, they bring in fire trucks with a hydraulically powered, extending ladder. Some of these ladders have a turntable base, so they can pivot in any direction, and built-in water pipes capable of delivering 1,000 gal (3,785 l) of water per minute to the top. Some turntable ladders have a "basket" at the top, big enough to hold up to three firefighters.

▶ This fire truck ladder has several sections that can extend to a height of more than 100 ft (30 …

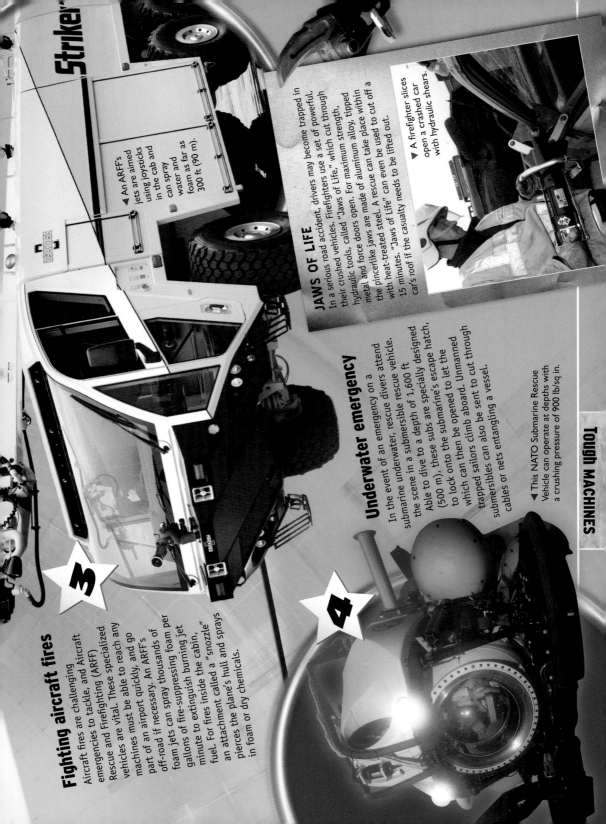

Striker

Fighting aircraft fires

Aircraft fires are challenging to tackle, and Aircraft Rescue and Firefighting (ARFF) emergencies are vital. These specialized vehicles must be able to reach any part of an airport quickly, and go off-road if necessary. An ARFF's foam jets can spray thousands of gallons of fire-suppressing foam per minute to extinguish the cabin. For fires inside the cabin, an attachment called a "snozzle" pierces the plane's hull and sprays in foam or dry chemicals.

3

▶ An ARFF's jets are aimed using joysticks in the cab and can spray water and foam as far as 300 ft (90 m).

JAWS OF LIFE

In a serious road accident, drivers may become trapped in their crushed vehicles. Firefighters use a set of powerful, hydraulic tools, called "Jaws of Life," which cut through metal and force doors open. For maximum strength, the pincerlike jaws are made of aluminum alloy, tipped with heat-treated steel. A rescue can take place within 15 minutes. "Jaws of Life" can even be used to cut off a car's roof if the casualty needs to be lifted out.

▶ A firefighter slices open a crashed car with hydraulic shears.

Underwater emergency

4

In the event of an emergency on a submarine underwater, rescue divers attend the scene in a submersible rescue vehicle. Able to dive to a depth of 1,600 ft (500 m), these subs are specially designed to lock onto the submarine's escape hatch, which can then be opened to let the trapped sailors climb aboard. Unmanned submersibles can also be sent to cut through cables or nets entangling a vessel.

▶ This NATO Submarine Rescue Vehicle can operate at depths with a crushing pressure of 900 lb/sq in.

SUBZERO
Heroes

Deep snow and thick ice stop most vehicles dead in their tracks. If you want to keep moving in the coldest places on Earth, you'll need a machine that's up to the subzero challenge. Icebreaker ships and planes with skis are more than a match for polar ice. And if you need to clear a path through deep snow, a snowplow or blower is just the job.

▶ The steel hull of the icebreaker *Yamal* is 1–2 in (2.5–5 cm) thick. It can drive its way through the Arctic sea ice on its journey to the North Pole.

Icebreaker ships

In the polar regions, where icebergs drift and seawater freezes, icebreakers are the only ships that can operate. A strengthened steel hull, sloping bow, and powerful engines enable an icebreaker to smash a path through thick sea ice. Russian nuclear-powered icebreakers such as the *Yamal* are the most powerful in the world. They can forge a path through ice that is up to 16 ft (5 m) thick.

Cut and blow

From driveways to runways, specialized vehicles called snow blowers clear deep snow in no time. As the vehicle drives forward, a series of blades in a rotating drum slice up the snow and pull it into the machine. The snow is then blown out of a chute on the top of the vehicle, hurling it many feet away.

◀ A large snow blower can clear up to 11 million lb (5,000 tons) of snow an hour and blow it 150 ft (46 m) away.

Snow on the rails

When snow piles up on railroad tracks, snowplows are the machines to clear it. The simplest railroad snowplow has a wedge-shaped front, which forces the snow aside as the train speeds along. For the deepest snow, a rotary snowplow with spinning blades is used. The blades cut through deep, hard-packed snowdrifts, removing them from the tracks.

◄ A rotary snowplow's blades spin more than 100 times per minute, shredding the hardest snow to powder.

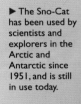 ► The Sno-Cat has been used by scientists and explorers in the Arctic and Antarctic since 1951, and is still in use today.

Making tracks

Normal cars and trucks would get stuck in the deep snow of the polar regions, so tracked vehicles are the transport of choice for this frozen wilderness. Their wide, ribbed tracks not only spread their weight, stopping them from sinking in soft snow, but they also provide grip. As well as carrying personnel, these vehicles can tow sleds laden with up to 8 tons of equipment.

▼ A ski-equipped LC-130 takes off from an ice runway in Antarctica. Its two main skis are 20 ft (6 m) long and 5.5 ft (1.7 m) wide.

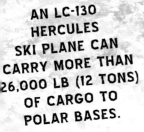

AN LC-130 HERCULES SKI PLANE CAN CARRY MORE THAN 26,000 LB (12 TONS) OF CARGO TO POLAR BASES.

Polar plane

At the poles, where snow and ice cover every solid surface, an airplane is the last vehicle you may expect to see. However, the LC-130 Hercules is a regular visitor. A fleet of LC-130s ferry scientists and equipment between research stations and camps in Antarctica. Their ski-equipped landing gear means that they can land on snow and ice.

Beneath the hood, under the wing, and below deck, some of the most powerful engines can be found. Jet engines propel airliners through the atmosphere at just below the speed of sound and rockets thrust space vehicles into orbit. Back on Earth, piston engines boost supercars to incredible speeds and power colossal ships across the oceans.

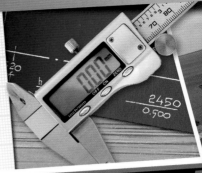

Superhot jets

The most advanced airliner engines, such as the Rolls-Royce Trent XWB, are remarkable machines. They power heavy aircraft laden with hundreds of passengers, thousands of miles around the world. They generate enormous thrust simply by compressing air, then heating it to make it expand. In fact, the air becomes so hot that it could melt the engine! These engines have to be designed carefully to withstand the incredible pressures generated inside the engine, and with clever cooling technology to stop overheating.

BYPASS AIR
90 percent of air sucked in by the fan bypasses the combustor, flows around it, and goes out the back of the engine. This produces most of the thrust.

	1 FAN	2 COMPRESSOR	3 COMBUSTOR
Pressure:	15 lb/sq in	120 lb/sq in	500 lb/sq in
Temperature:	176°F (80°C)	554°F (290°C)	2,700°F (1,480°C)

1 FAN
The fan sucks large quantities of air into the engine. Its blades are made of titanium.

FAN CASING
The casing surrounding the fan stops broken fan blades from flying out of the engine.

2 COMPRESSOR
The compressor is made up of many rotating, bladed fans. It squashes air to one fiftieth of its original volume.

3 COMBUSTOR
Inside this heat-resistant chamber, fuel is mixed with the air and ignited, creating high-energy expanding gases

2450
0.500

Emma Maersk

MARINE MAMMOTH

The biggest cargo ships are powered by diesel engines the size of a house. The Emma Maersk is one of the biggest containerships ever built. To propel it across the ocean, it needs a massively powerful engine—the Wärtsilä RT-flex96C. This huge powerplant is 90 ft (27 m) long, 44 ft (13.5 m) high, and weighs a staggering 5.1 million lb (2,300 tons).

The RT-flex96C engine is the world's biggest diesel engine and powers the 1,300-ft- (400-m-) long containership, the Emma Maersk.

Koenigsegg Agera R

SWEDISH SUPERCAR

The most powerful street-legal cars pack ten times the power of a small family car. One such supercar, the Swedish-made Koenigsegg Agera R, has a 1,140-hp engine hidden under its sleek, streamlined body. This superpowerful engine and the car's carefully designed shape give the Agera R a 0–60 mph (0–97 km/h) time of 2.9 seconds and a top speed of 273 mph (440 km/h).

Airbus A350

4 TURBINE
The turbine spins at 10,000 rpm, powered by the jet of hot air leaving the engine.

4 TURBINE
500–900 lb/sq in
2,000–2,700°F (1,090–1,480°C)

HOT AIR
The air expands as it heats up and rushes out of the engine.

The Airbus A350 is powered by two Rolls-Royce Trent XWB engines. Each engine has 18,000 parts that have to work together seamlessly.

Saturn V

Each F-1 rocket engine burns 670 gal (2,540 l) of kerosene and liquid oxygen every second.

FABULOUS F-1

The Saturn V rocket that launched astronauts to the Moon weighed more than 6 million lb (2,700 tons). The most powerful rocket engines ever built got it off the ground—Rocketdyne F-1s. Each F-1 was 19 ft (5.8 m) long and weighed more than 9 tons. They had to withstand kerosene burning inside them at a temperature of 5,970°F (3,300°C).

Tough MACHINES

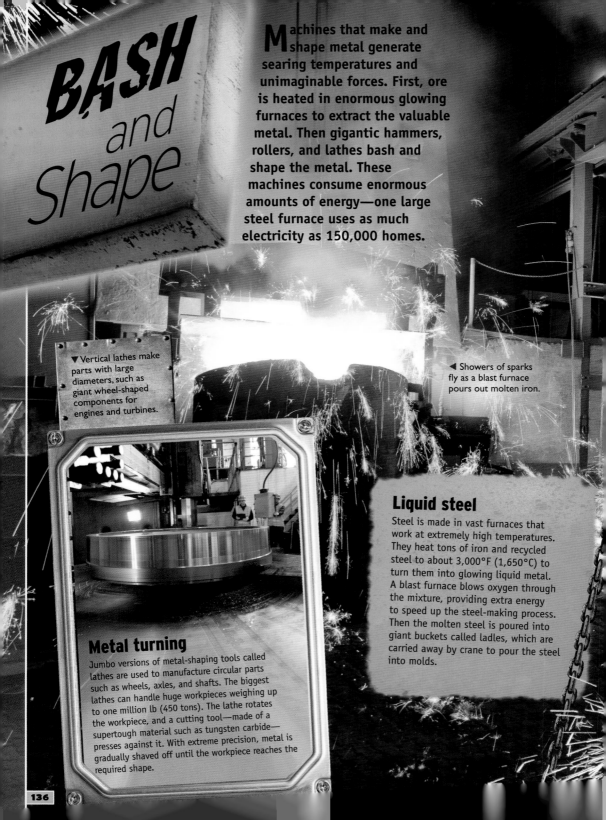

BASH and Shape

Machines that make and shape metal generate searing temperatures and unimaginable forces. First, ore is heated in enormous glowing furnaces to extract the valuable metal. Then gigantic hammers, rollers, and lathes bash and shape the metal. These machines consume enormous amounts of energy—one large steel furnace uses as much electricity as 150,000 homes.

▼ Vertical lathes make parts with large diameters, such as giant wheel-shaped components for engines and turbines.

◄ Showers of sparks fly as a blast furnace pours out molten iron.

Liquid steel

Steel is made in vast furnaces that work at extremely high temperatures. They heat tons of iron and recycled steel to about 3,000°F (1,650°C) to turn them into glowing liquid metal. A blast furnace blows oxygen through the mixture, providing extra energy to speed up the steel-making process. Then the molten steel is poured into giant buckets called ladles, which are carried away by crane to pour the steel into molds.

Metal turning

Jumbo versions of metal-shaping tools called lathes are used to manufacture circular parts such as wheels, axles, and shafts. The biggest lathes can handle huge workpieces weighing up to one million lb (450 tons). The lathe rotates the workpiece, and a cutting tool—made of a supertough material such as tungsten carbide—presses against it. With extreme precision, metal is gradually shaved off until the workpiece reaches the required shape.

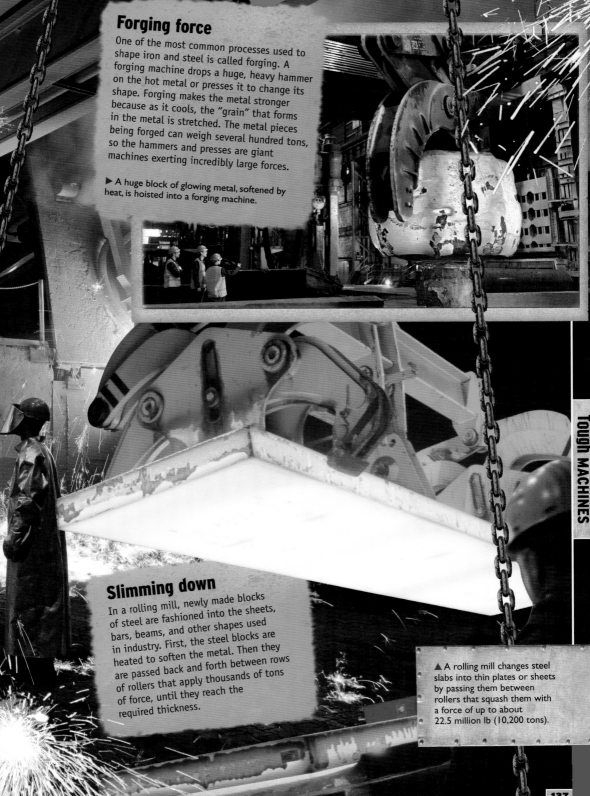

Forging force

One of the most common processes used to shape iron and steel is called forging. A forging machine drops a huge, heavy hammer on the hot metal or presses it to change its shape. Forging makes the metal stronger because as it cools, the "grain" that forms in the metal is stretched. The metal pieces being forged can weigh several hundred tons, so the hammers and presses are giant machines exerting incredibly large forces.

▶ A huge block of glowing metal, softened by heat, is hoisted into a forging machine.

Slimming down

In a rolling mill, newly made blocks of steel are fashioned into the sheets, bars, beams, and other shapes used in industry. First, the steel blocks are heated to soften the metal. Then they are passed back and forth between rows of rollers that apply thousands of tons of force, until they reach the required thickness.

▲ A rolling mill changes steel slabs into thin plates or sheets by passing them between rollers that squash them with a force of up to about 22.5 million lb (10,200 tons).

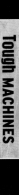

CAR CRUSHERS

Every year, millions of cars reach the end of their useful life, and a lineup of specialized metal-crunching machines help to dispose of them. First, vehicles are dismantled to recover and recycle useful parts and metals. Then machines crush them down, chew them up, and spit them out as scrap metal.

▲ A scrapyard grab punches through a car's body and picks it up as if it were a toy.

Step 1: GRIP!

Scrapped cars are picked up, moved around the scrapyard, and loaded into crushing and shredding machines by huge hydraulic grippers called grabs. The grab opens and closes like an outsize steel hand, and is able to lift up to 9 tons of weight. A grab can be fitted to the arm of a crane, or to an excavator's boom instead of a digging bucket.

THE LARGEST SHREDDER IN THE WORLD—THE LYNXS AT THE SIMS PLANT, SOUTH WALES—CAN SHRED 450 CARS PER HOUR.

RECYCLING SAVINGS

The recycling of vehicles is a multibillion dollar industry, because it recovers valuable materials such as metals. Recycled steel and iron don't need to be made from new. Every car recycled saves one ton of metal-containing rock called ore, and 1,400 lb (635 kg) of coal needed to process the ore.

An average car contains more than:
2,000 lb (907 kg) of steel
240 lb (110 kg) of aluminum
110 lb (50 kg) of rubber
50 lb (23 kg) of carbon
42 lb (19 kg) of copper
41 lb (18 kg) of silicon
22 lb (10 kg) of zinc

Step 2: CRUSH!

When fuel, oil, batteries, glass, and other useful parts have been removed from scrapped cars, the car bodies are crushed in a hydraulic press. These powerful machines can exert crushing forces of up to 336,000 lb (150 tons) to squash car bodies flat. Another type of crusher compresses them into refrigerator-sized blocks called bales. This makes the cars easier to store and transport by truck to a recycling plant.

▼ A hydraulic crushing plate bears down with enormous force, pressing a car to less than half its original size.

◄ Large car recycling plants can process up to 110 million lb (50,000 tons) of material per month.

▼ Rotors in the shredder spin at 175 mph (280 km/h), tearing cars to pieces.

Step 3: SHRED!

The compacted car bodies are fed into the "mouth" of a shredding machine. A series of heavy hammers on spinning rotors tear the car bodies into pieces smaller than a fist, which are carried along a conveyor belt to be sorted. Magnets separate the iron and steel from other metals and fans blow light plastic and cloth away. Finally, devices called eddy current separators sort the remaining metals from nonmetals by using electric currents.

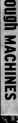

Tough MACHINES

RUGGED Robots

When a job is too dangerous for people, specially designed robots are readied for the task. They can search for survivors in unsafe disaster areas, investigate locations with lethal radiation levels, and operate in the airless void of space. When it comes to bomb disposal, the Police and Armed Forces' robot workforce carry out these high-risk missions.

TEODor
Job: Bomb disposal
Made by: Telerob, Germany
Special feature: Can be fitted with up to six cameras and armed with weapons and tools to deal with unexploded bombs

Robot rescuer

T-52 Enryu was designed to aid rescue in earthquake-hit zones. The robot stands 11 ft (3 m) tall and is strong enough to lift a car. It has two eight-jointed arms with claw attachments, which can lift debris to clear a path for a rescue team to reach possible survivors. Enryu is controlled by an operator in a cockpit inside the robot or, if this is too dangerous, using a control box from a safe distance.

T-52 ENRYU
Job: Aids rescue in disaster areas
Made by: Tmsuk, Japan
Special skill: Its two 20-ft- (6-m-) long arms can lift a combined weight of one ton

Intrepid assistant

TEODor is a small, tracked vehicle used by law enforcement agencies worldwide to dispose of explosives. Its tracks enable it to travel on rough terrain, and it is small enough to maneuver inside a house. TEODor is equipped with cameras, a movable arm, and specialized tools to investigate and disarm an explosive device. The robot is remotely controlled by an operator a safe distance away, who sees the robot's view through its cameras.

Volcano explorer

Active volcano craters may be searingly hot and full of toxic gases, but volcanologists prize samples collected from them to study past eruptions and predict future activity. In 1993, a walking robot called *Dante II* was developed to gather these samples. It had eight legs and, attached to an anchor cable, could rappel down sheer, uneven crater walls. When the target was reached, *Dante II* took samples and recorded measurements with its onboard instruments, and relayed data to controllers via satellite.

DANTE II

Job: Explore active volcano craters
Made by: Carnegie Mellon University, U.S.
Special skill: Can rappel down crater walls and walk over objects up to 3 ft (one meter) high

Space station robot

Since 2008, the International Space Station (ISS) has had a two-armed robot called the Special Purpose Dexterous Manipulator, or Dextre, on board. It's a "handyman" that works in the deadly conditions outside the ISS, especially in the great extremes of temperature—boiling hot in sunshine and freezing cold in shadow.

DEXTRE

Job: Maintenance of the ISS
Made by: MacDonald, Dettwiler, and Associates, Canada
Special feature: Two 11-ft- (3-m-) long robotic arms, equipped with tools

Robot investigator

Packbots are small enough to fit in a backpack and able to deal with a range of risky tasks. These robots are designed to withstand rough treatment—a Packbot can survive a 6-ft (1.8-m) drop onto concrete without damage. Treaded tracks help it climb over obstacles and can flip it upright if it is overturned. Following the 2011 Japanese tsunami, two Packbots were sent into Fukushima nuclear power plant to inspect its damaged reactors. The robots worked in high levels of radiation and sent back live video and temperature recordings.

PACKBOT

Job: Investigation and bomb disposal in dangerous locations
Made by: iRobot, U.S.
Special skills: Small, tough, and adaptable

FAR-OUT Explorers

Space is a hostile environment. Spacecraft have to be able to survive conditions that would freeze or fry most machines on Earth. They must also keep working for many years—*Voyager 1* has been sending back data from its journey to the edge of the Solar System for more than 35 years.

A curious craft

The *Curiosity* rover landed on Mars in August 2012 to investigate if the planet once supported tiny life-forms. Temperatures on Mars are cold, so a heating system warms the rover, keeping its instruments operational. Six 20-in- (50-cm-) diameter wheels allow *Curiosity* to traverse rough terrain. It can collect samples for testing by scooping up soil or using its robotic arm to grind into rocks.

▼ The *Curiosity* rover is a nuclear-powered electric vehicle the size of a small car

▲ The SOHO spacecraft generates electricity for its instruments from sunlight using its 31-ft- (9.5-m-) long solar panel array.

Studying the Sun

Storms on the Sun can affect us on Earth, so scientists are keen to study our nearest star. The Solar and Heliospheric Observatory (SOHO) spacecraft has been observing the Sun since 1996. It orbits a point in space about 930,000 mi (1.5 million km) away from Earth, where its instruments have an uninterrupted view of the Sun.

MERCURY

VENUS

EARTH

MARS

Planetary messenger

Mercury, the closest planet to the Sun, is being studied by the spacecraft *Messenger*. *Messenger* has to cope with temperatures as high as 700°F (370°C) and its instruments and electronics are kept at room temperature by a sunshade made of heat-resistant ceramic cloth. This also protects the craft from solar radiation.

◄ *Messenger* was launched in 2004 and went into orbit around the planet in 2011.

Frozen spacefarer

In 2006, a spacecraft called *New Horizons* was launched on a mission to the distant dwarf planet, Pluto. It is set to arrive in 2015. To cope with the intense cold at Pluto, *New Horizons* is covered with multiple layers of insulation. This is so effective at conserving heat that the craft had to cool itself while traveling through the inner Solar System to prevent it overheating.

▶ *New Horizons* has to withstand temperatures as low as -390°F (-234°C) at the edge of the Solar System.

PLUTO

NEPTUNE

SATURN

JUPITER

URANUS

Titan
(moon)

Titan lander

As the *Cassini* spacecraft hurtled toward the ringed planet Saturn in 2004, it released a mini probe called *Huygens*, headed for Saturn's biggest moon, Titan. Very little was known about Titan, so *Huygens* had to be able to land on any surface, solid or liquid. It descended through Titan's thick atmosphere before bouncing and skidding to a stop, taking photographs on the way down and for 90 minutes after landing.

SPACECRAFT THAT EXPLORE THE OUTER PLANETS ARE POWERED BY NUCLEAR ENERGY, BECAUSE THEY TRAVEL TOO FAR FROM THE SUN TO USE SOLAR POWER.

2 *Parachute slows descent*

1 *Heat shield is released and instruments are activated before touchdown*

3 *Huygens lands on surface of Titan at a speed of 16 ft/sec (5 m/sec)*

▶ The *Huygens* probe descended 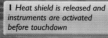 through Titan's cloudy atmosphere by parachute.

DEEPEST DIVERS

Some of the most extreme conditions on Earth are found at the bottom of the ocean. The deepest parts of the ocean floor are 7 mi (11 km) below the surface and the pressure exceeds 16,000 lb/sq in. It is also freezing cold—just over 32°F (0°C)—and totally dark. Only the toughest submersibles can operate here.

DIVING ARMOR

Divers can descend to depths of more than 2,000 ft (610 m) wearing an Atmospheric Diving Suit (ADS). It is a jointed suit of armor, reinforced to withstand crushing water pressure 60 times higher than at the surface. Inside the suit, the pressure is the same as on the surface, so the diver can breathe normally with no risk of decompression sickness, known as "the bends."

▼ This French Navy rescue diver is wearing an ADS called a Newtsuit. A thruster backpack can propel the diver through the water.

Underwater flier

DeepFlight Challenger "flies" through the water like a plane, using upside-down wings to descend at a speed of 350 ft (110 m) per minute. To withstand the pressure at the deepest part of the ocean its slender hull is made of supertough carbon fiber and the viewing dome is made of quartz. Despite *DeepFlight Challenger* being relatively light at 3.5 tons, it is able to dive to the seafloor and return to the surface in only five hours.

▲ Aquanauts including Sir Richard Branson plan to dive to the deepest parts of the world's five oceans in a *DeepFlight Challenger* submersible.

BELOW 3,300 FT (1,000 M), THE OCEAN IS PITCH BLACK

144

Robot sub

In 2009, *Nereus* became the third vehicle ever to explore Challenger Deep—the deepest point in the ocean. The unmanned submersible is made of light, ceramic material, which can endure huge pressures. It descended all the way to the seafloor trailing a hair-thin optical fiber, up to 25 mi (40 km) long, which was attached to a ship on the surface. This allowed *Nereus* to send back live video and images to the surface.

▲ The 3-ton submersible, *Nereus*, is powered by onboard battery packs, which enable it to stay submerged for up to 24 hours.

In design

The *36000* looks like an alien spaceship, but it's a submersible being built by Triton Submarines to take people to the deepest parts of the ocean. Its occupants—up to three people—will sit inside a thick glass dome, which becomes stronger the more pressure it is put under. It will be used by scientists for deep-ocean research and tourists who want to visit the deep-sea world.

▼ Triton's *36000* descends at 500 ft (150 m) per minute, reaching the deepest part of the ocean within about 75 minutes.

CHALLENGER DEEP—36,069 FT (10,994 M) BELOW SEA LEVEL—IS THE DEEPEST PLACE ON EARTH.

Deep-sea challenge

Movie director James Cameron is the third person to visit Challenger Deep, located at the bottom of the Mariana Trench in the Pacific Ocean, 36,069 ft (10,994 m) down. He made the journey in a submersible called *Deepsea Challenger*. Cameron sat inside a 2.5-in-(7.3-cm-) thick spherical steel chamber, housed in the 24-ft- (7-m-) tall craft, and looked out through a tiny viewport.

▲ *Deepsea Challenger* reached the deepest part of the ocean on March 26, 2012. Its 43-in (110-cm) crew sphere is big enough for just one person.

Sea Defenders

The forces of nature are formidable. Storm surges and exceptionally high tides can overwhelm coastal cities, and rising sea levels are making this problem worse. Mammoth mechanical barriers protect some of the world's biggest ports from flooding.

THE THAMES BARRIER

The U.K.'s capital city, London, is protected from flooding by a barrier across the River Thames, which flows through the city. The Thames Barrier's ten steel gates span 1,706 ft (520 m) from bank to bank. The four biggest gates in the middle weigh 7 million lb (3,200 tons) each.

Pier roof
Made of timber covered with stainless steel sheets to protect machinery inside

Rocking arm
Moved by two hydraulic cylinders in the pier roof to rotate the gate

▶ The barrier can protect London from a surge up to 7 ft (2 m) high, and to date the barrier has never been breached.

Rising sector gate
Made of 2-in- (5-cm-) thick high-strength steel, designed to allow water and air in and out

Central pier
Each central concrete pier is 36 ft (11 m) wide, 210 ft (65 m) long, and penetrates 50 ft (15 m) into the riverbed

PROTECTING LONDON

When "open," the Thames Barrier's gates lie flat on the riverbed in a curved trough. When forecasters predict the threat of flood, boat traffic on the river is ordered to stop and the machinery on the piers starts up. The hydraulic rocking arms rotate the gates, which rise up from the riverbed until they stand vertical. This forms an impassable barrier, keeping the surge of seawater out of London. When the threat passes, the machinery rotates the gates back and they disappear below the waves.

Gate rotates 90 degrees to stand upright and hold back a storm surge.

Tunnels
A pair of tunnels run beneath the Thames, providing access and services

Filter layer
A layer of stone blocks stops the riverbed from being washed away

Gravel layer
A deep layer of gravel laid over solid chalk bed

Sinking city

The Italian city of Venice is world-famous for its canals. It also suffers from frequent flooding. To make matters worse, Venice is slowly sinking into the mud it is built on. Engineers are laying 78 gates on the bed of the lagoon that surrounds the city. When the gates are closed, the lagoon will be sealed off from the sea. The project is called M.O.S.E. (Modulo Sperimentale Elettromeccanico), and is due to be completed in 2014.

◀ The gates that protect Venice are closed by pumping air into them. This makes them buoyant, so they stand upright.

▼ Each of the gates of Rotterdam's Maeslant barrier is 787 ft (240 m) long and 72 ft (22 m) high.

Floating giants

Rotterdam in the Netherlands is one of the world's busiest ports. If high sea levels pose a threat, the two huge steel gates of the Maeslant barrier—each the weight of two Eiffel Towers—seal the city off from the North Sea. Open, the gates sit in dry docks in the waterway walls. When needed, they are floated out until they meet. Then they are flooded with water to weigh them down.

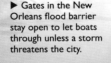

▶ Gates in the New Orleans flood barrier stay open to let boats through unless a storm threatens the city.

SOUTHERN BRITAIN IS SLOWLY SINKING, INCREASING THE FLOODING RISK IN LONDON.

Storm barriers for New Orleans

In 2005, New Orleans, U.S., was devastated by a flood caused by Hurricane Katrina. Since then, the city's flood defenses have been rebuilt and improved. New Orleans is now protected by the world's largest storm surge barrier—a wall 2 mi (3.2 km) long and 32 ft (10 m) high, fortified with 350 mi (560 km) of embankments called levees. Rainfall and floodwater can also be pumped out of the city by the world's most powerful pumping station.

Harsh LANDS

All over the planet, people have discovered ingenious ways to not only survive in extreme environments, but to positively thrive.

◀ The sun beats down on fishermen perched on stilts that are fixed into the ocean floor in Ahangama, Sri Lanka.

Scorched Dry

Hot deserts cover about 14 percent of Earth's surface. Biggest and hottest of all is the Sahara—about 3,630,000 sq mi (9,400,000 sq km) of baking sand, gravel, and rock, where the temperature has been known to reach 131°F (55°C). Desert peoples have spent thousands of years learning how to survive in these trackless wastes, where shelter and water is perilously hard to find.

The desert people

Camels are perfectly adapted for survival in a desert environment, but humans face tough challenges traveling in seriously hot, dry conditions. The head may be protected from the fierce heat with a long scarf, and during a sandstorm this can be wrapped around the eyes and nose to protect against grit and dust. Loose robes keep the body cool and protected from the Sun's scorching glare.

▼ Tuareg people—camel herders and traders who live in an area of North and West Africa—haul much-needed water from a desert well.

▼ A woman collects ground water from a well in the Kalahari desert in Botswana.

The big thirst

Deep beneath many hot deserts, trapped in porous rocks, there are ancient reserves of water. The challenge is how to reach them. It is difficult enough with drills and modern machinery, but many desert peoples have only the most basic tools. They must hack out deep shafts and channels, which may cave in at any moment, risking their lives to bring water to their community.

A splash in the desert

Well shafts and tunnels can help to supply a desert waterhole, or oasis. These allow thirsty goats or camels to drink their fill. The water is also used to irrigate plots where crops and date palms can be grown. Shade reduces evaporation, while roots anchor the desert soil and trap moisture.

MANY PLANTS STORE WATER. AUSTRALIA'S ABORIGINES TAKE DRINKING WATER FROM THE ROOTS OF THE RED MALLEE EUCALYPTUS.

▲ This vegetable garden at Chirfa, in Niger, is watered by a 16-ft- (5-m-) deep well.

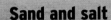

Desert stalkers

The San people or "Bushmen" live in the Kalahari desert of southern Africa. They are experts at survival during the dry season, when times are hard. Some hunt desert animals and gather roots and berries. They may eat locusts, caterpillars, termites, beetles, and snakes. Water can be stored in ostrich eggshells.

▶ A San boy from the Kalahari sips water from a cavity in a tree, using a grass straw.

Sand and salt

Many deserts are rich in minerals, but extracting and transporting them in scorching conditions is dangerous and difficult. Salt has been traded across the Sahara for many centuries and is still carried by camel caravans today. In northeast Africa, salt is mined in the Danakil desert. At Lake Assal, evaporation by the burning sun is so intense that the minerals in the water become highly concentrated—the lake is ten times saltier than the sea.

▶ Salt is a precious desert commodity.

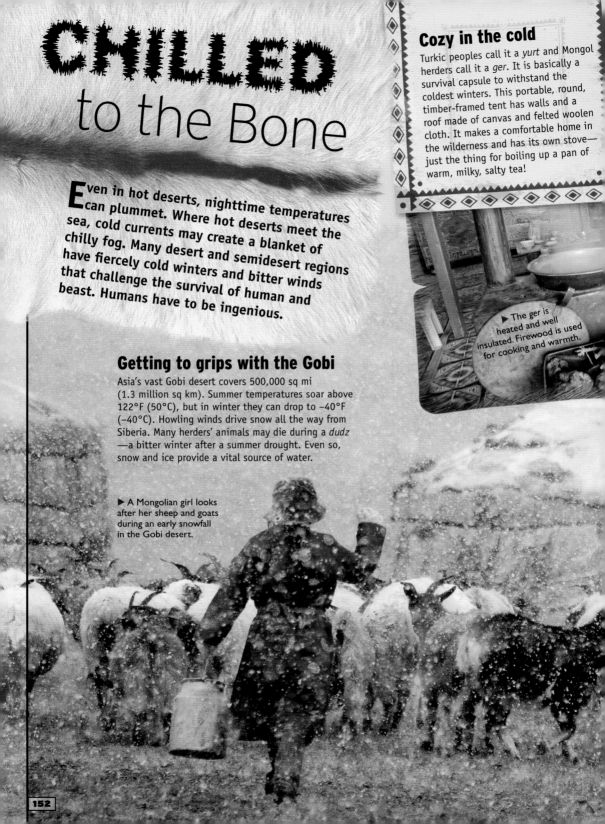

CHILLED
to the Bone

Even in hot deserts, nighttime temperatures can plummet. Where hot deserts meet the sea, cold currents may create a blanket of chilly fog. Many desert and semidesert regions have fiercely cold winters and bitter winds that challenge the survival of human and beast. Humans have to be ingenious.

Cozy in the cold

Turkic peoples call it a *yurt* and Mongol herders call it a *ger*. It is basically a survival capsule to withstand the coldest winters. This portable, round, timber-framed tent has walls and a roof made of canvas and felted woolen cloth. It makes a comfortable home in the wilderness and has its own stove—just the thing for boiling up a pan of warm, milky, salty tea!

▶ The ger is heated and well insulated. Firewood is used for cooking and warmth.

Getting to grips with the Gobi

Asia's vast Gobi desert covers 500,000 sq mi (1.3 million sq km). Summer temperatures soar above 122°F (50°C), but in winter they can drop to –40°F (–40°C). Howling winds drive snow all the way from Siberia. Many herders' animals may die during a *dudz* —a bitter winter after a summer drought. Even so, snow and ice provide a vital source of water.

▶ A Mongolian girl looks after her sheep and goats during an early snowfall in the Gobi desert.

A foggy harvest

Chile's Atacama isn't the coldest desert, but it is the driest. Some parts have seen no rain in centuries. The icy waters of the Pacific Ocean's Humboldt Current cool the desert air, causing dense fog to roll inland. Water vapor condenses on desert cacti and lichens, providing drops of moisture for birds and animals. Humans have tried to mimic this process by stringing up giant nets to trap the water vapor for human use.

▼ Droplets that form on the nets drain off into pipes, which lead to a reservoir.

Twin humps

The tamed Bactrian camel is man's best friend in the steppes and cold deserts of Central Asia, Mongolia, and China. Its shaggy winter coat keeps it warm. Its long eyelashes and nostrils keep out the summer dust. Its broad feet can pad over soft sand or sharp gravel. The two fatty humps provide reserves of nutrition. The powerful body of this superbeast can carry heavy loads over long distances.

▶ A nomadic Mongolian herder loads his ger onto a Bactrian camel.

Harsh Lands

153

Cruel ARCTIC

The Arctic is one of the most severe environments in which humans have ever settled. It is a wilderness of bitter cold, blizzards, and treacherous ice, and in midwinter the darkness lasts all day and night. The Arctic climate is now changing, but even this presents the peoples of the Arctic with new threats to their survival, as the animals they hunt are also at risk.

▼ An Inuit from the Canadian Arctic builds up the roof of an igloo.

Shelters in the snow

Today the Inuit live in modern houses, prefabricated from timber and imported. Traditional homes included low dugout shelters of stone, turf, or whalebone, and tents of caribou hide. The temporary lodge made from blocks of wind-hardened snow, known as an igloo, can still be made by hunters using ancient skills.

Keeping out the cold

The Inuit today wear modern clothes against the bitter cold, as they are convenient to buy and wear. Little can beat a multilayered traditional outfit when it comes to preventing the body losing vital warmth. Shirts, hoodies, breeches, socks, boots, and gloves can be stitched from bird and hare skins, sealskin, caribou hide, polar bear fur, or fox fur.

◄ Traditional slit glasses prevent "snow blindness," caused by reflected dazzle.

Speeding across the ice

Traditional Inuit transport was a wooden sled, pulled by up to 14 huskies. With a top speed of about 20 mph (32 km/h), it was used to carry people or goods. The design varied from one region to the next, depending on whether it was used to cross sea ice, powdery snow, or packed snow. Dog sleds are still used today, but the standard way of getting about in the Arctic is by sturdy snowmobile.

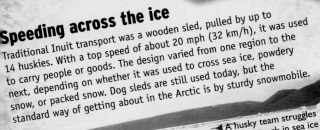

◀ A husky team struggles to cross a crack in sea ice in northwestern Greenland.

BODY HEAT INSIDE AN IGLOO MEANS THE TEMPERATURE WITHIN RARELY DIPS BELOW 60°F (16°C), EVEN WHEN IT'S -40°F (-40°C) OUTSIDE.

Haul it up!

The Arctic Ocean is a vital resource for survival, providing food for hunting and fishing communities. The sea around the North Pole is frozen all year round, but outer regions melt briefly in summer. Hunters wait beside holes in the ice to harpoon seals as they come up for air. Fishermen cut holes in the ice to catch fish. The line may drop 500 ft (150 m) or more to haul up halibut or Atlantic wolffish.

▲ An Inuit fishes for Arctic cod near Igloolik, Nunavut.

▶ A Sami woman from Norway wears traditional costume as she rounds up reindeer.

Reindeer people

Reindeer have long provided a livelihood for peoples such as the Sami, Nenets, and Evenki, who live in the harsh terrain of the Eurasian Arctic. Some families still follow their herds each year along ancient migration routes, crossing rivers and braving blizzards. Many animals help humans survive in extreme environments. Semitame reindeer provide Arctic communities with meat, milk, hide, and antler horn. They can also pull sleds through the snowy wastelands.

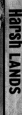

Raw JUNGLE

Dense foliage, sweltering humidity, insects that bite without mercy—a tropical forest is a formidable foe. As loggers move in, our opportunities to preserve these precious places may be running out. Forest peoples have been benefitting from their valuable resources for thousands of years.

Rain forest healers

Many peoples have learned to survive in the depths of forests by making potions and remedies from the plants that grow there. We now know that many of these plants have great value as medicines. The cashew tree, which comes from Brazil, has a nutshell that is antibacterial. The bark is soaked or boiled to stop diarrhea, and the seed is ground to treat snakebite.

▶ A Yagua healer, from the Javari River region of Peru, strips bark from a tree to make medicines.

ARROWS AND DARTS TIPPED WITH GOLDEN FROG POISON HELP HUNTERS KILL ANIMALS FOR FOOD IN REMOTE FOREST VILLAGES.

Frog poison!

What is small, bright yellow, and lives in hot and humid jungles in South America? The golden poison frog, also known as *Phyllobates terribilis*. Glands in its skin produce a deadly poison that protects it from predators. The Embera people, from the Choco region of Colombia, carefully smear this fluid on arrows and blowpipe darts, and they remain poisonous for up to three years. The Embera's prey includes monkeys and deer.

▶ Each frog produces one milligram of lethal poison—enough to kill 10–20 humans!

The high life

The Korowai people, who live in Papua, build their houses in the forest canopy. They construct a strong platform on a wanbom or banyan tree, and sago fronds tied with raffia provide a roof. This treehouse can be home to a dozen people. In the past, building high off the ground was believed to protect the family from evil spirits, and it prevented attacks from warlike neighbors. Today it still offers relief—from the swarming mosquitoes down below.

◀ Korowai houses may tower 115 ft (35 m) above the jungle floor.

Dinner for the Baka

Small groups of Baka hunters live in Africa, in the rain forests of the Congo Republic, Gabon, and Cameroon. The forest provides them with plentiful nuts, berries, fruits, wild yams, mushrooms, caterpillars, and protein-rich termites. Rivers are dammed to catch fish and the men laboriously hunt monkeys and forest antelopes.

▲ A Bangladeshi man smokes wild bees from their nest in the forest. The reward? Sweet, golden honeycomb—worth a few stings!

FOREST PEOPLE THREATENED

In a remote area on the border between Peru and Brazil lives an isolated tribe of Panoan Indians, who have had little or no contact with the outside world. Their survival is not threatened by the rain forest environment but by the savagery of intruders who cut down trees and poison rivers.

◀ A small group of forest-dwelling Panoan Indians stare up at an aircraft.

SEARING
Savanna

The African savanna is wide-open land under a raging sun. The tawny grasslands are dotted with patches of scrub, flat-topped thorny acacia trees, and rocky outcrops. These plains teem with the last great herds of wild animals on Earth. Lions hunt zebra and wildebeest, and hyenas and vultures scavenge at the kills. Humans have developed clever ways to survive in this merciless environment.

A Himba woman, covered in red ochre, goes to milk the cows penned in the stockade.

In the land of the Masai

The Masai people live on the Kenyan and Tanzanian savanna. Each family home is based upon a small, round structure, made by weaving branches around poles. Any gaps are plugged with grass and leaves. When the structure is complete the hut is covered with a render of cow dung, ash, and mud to make it waterproof.

This way of life has been threatened in recent years by extreme and long droughts.

Behind the stockade

A stockade is a barrier of thorns or sticks used by savanna peoples. Its purpose is to keep herds penned in and keep cattle thieves or wild animals out. A stockade and a hut settlement is central to the way of life for the seminomadic Himba people, who live in the dry northwes of Namibia. Their survival has been threatened by long years of warfare and fierce droughts, but they have managed to maintain their culture and traditions.

A tree for survival

The flat-topped acacia, or umbrella thorn, is a typical tree of the African savanna. It is tough, resistant to drought, and protected by thorns. The tree's pods and leaves provide food for livestock and various medicines. The wood is used to make weapons, tools, and stockades, while the fiber of the bark provides string and tannin for treating leather.

A Turkana boy in Kenya knocks down seed pods from an acacia tree to feed his hungry goats.

Knowing how to kindle a flame is a basic survival technique, and an important skill to have in the savanna.

Making sparks

To start a fire in the traditional way, a Masai herder places a softwood stick between the palms of his hands, fitting its end into a hole bored in a piece of hardwood. He rotates the stick rapidly. The friction makes the stick hot and charred, and when placed in a handful of straw, this kindling bursts into flame.

Blood and milk

The Masai and their northern cousins, the Samburu, herd cattle to provide themselves with milk and yogurt. Traditionally they also drink nutritious cow's blood during the dry season. They use an arrow to make a notch in the cow's vein and then seal it with ash. They may mix blood or milk in cornmeal to make a porridge. Cows also supply the community with meat, hides, leather thongs, horn, hoof, and even urine, which is used as a cleanser.

To many peoples of the savanna, cattle mean wealth, status, and nutrition.

Seas of GRASS

Throughout history humans have worked to make use of the world's grasslands. They have ridden trails into remote country, broken in wild horses, and reared cattle to graze the windswept pastures. They have struggled through tall prairie grasses up to 6 ft (2 m) high, and toiled to plant cereal crops.

THE COWBOY LIFESTYLE WAS TOTALLY DEPENDENT ON THE RESOURCES OF THE GREAT PLAINS—FOOD, CLOTHING, AND LIVELIHOODS ALL CAME FROM CATTLE.

The Gaucho legacy

The Pampas grasslands of South America cover an area of more than 290,000 sq mi (750,000 sq km). In the 1800s this wild terrain was the realm of bandits and gauchos—roaming groups of hardliving cowboys famous for their daredevil horsemanship. This way of life may have vanished, but horsemen still ride these grasslands. Large areas of the Pampas are now given over to crops—yet again, humans are adapting the world's grasslands to their needs.

◀ Together, man and horse have tamed the prairies.

Way out west

Cowboys played a legendary role in American history. Some still ride the range in the traditional way, even in the age of all-terrain vehicles. They move cattle to different pastures, round them up, brand them, and check fences and water supplies. They work in rugged back country and must be ready to deal with a rattlesnake or a mountain lion—they are tough people doing a tough job.

PLANET RABBIT

Some human interventions in the grasslands have been disastrous. The rabbit is a gentle, fluffy favorite, which is why British people took it to Australia. That was a very big mistake. In no time at all, these grass nibblers were destroying the environment, making native animal species extinct, and damaging crops on a massive scale.

PLAGUE PROPORTIONS!

1788	Rabbits brought to Australia from Britain
1859	24 rabbits released into the wild
1926	10 billion rabbits on the grasslands
1950s	99 percent of Australian rabbits killed by the disease myxomatosis. Just 40 years later, the population was up to 600 million

▲ Hunters (seen on horseback in the distance) round up rabbits for slaughter in a desperate attempt to control numbers.

◄ Part of a vanishing way of life, Gaucho Erasmo Betancur Casanova herds cattle on land in Patagonia, Argentina, which is due to become part of a national park.

The price of bread

Across the prairies of North America and the steppes of Eurasia, huge farms now cover the natural grasslands. Fleets of giant combine harvesters sweep over the landscape, gathering grain. In some parts of Africa and Asia, by contrast, producing grain still involves backbreaking human labor, with crops being harvested, threshed, winnowed, and milled by hand.

▲ An Ethiopian farmer winnows his crop, separating the edible part of the grain from the chaff.

MOUNTAIN
Menaces

Jagged peaks, snow-filled ravines, sheer rock faces, and fierce winds—the great mountain ranges are savage places for humans to venture. Yet for thousands of years hunters, traders, pilgrims, warriors, farmers, settlers, and builders of roads and railroads have risked their lives crossing high passes and climbing icy slopes—and many of them have relished the challenge.

Don't look down!

In the mountains, just getting from A to B is far from simple. In the Himalayas and the Andes, local people build simple rope bridges to span deep chasms and rushing river gorges. These high crossings enable people and goods to be carried to the other side, but to an outsider the swaying ropes and dizzying drop may be terrifying. Repairing and maintaining the bridges risks a fatal accident.

▶ People carefully cross a suspended footbridge that spans the Kali Gandaki gorge in Nepal.

White terror

Many villages in mountain valleys are in danger zones. Heavy falls of fresh snow may trigger a killer avalanche, sending snow roaring down the mountainside at speeds of up to 185 mph (300 km/h). Railroads and roads may be protected by tunnels or shelters. Trees, fences, or nets can act as barriers.

▶ Safety in the Alps—controlled blasts can prevent a dangerous buildup of snow on the upper slopes.

ABOUT ONE FIFTH OF EARTH'S SURFACE IS COVERED BY MOUNTAINS AND PLATEAUS. THESE AREAS ARE HOME TO MORE THAN 300 MILLION PEOPLE.

Top city

La Paz, Bolivia, is built at about 11,975 ft (3,650 m) above sea level. Some of its districts rise even higher into the Andes mountains. At this height, the air is "thin" (containing less oxygen). The local Quechua people have adapted to this over the ages, and their blood carries oxygen around the body with greater efficiency than that of people who are not used to living at high altitudes.

▶ La Paz is a city of 2.3 million inhabitants. Unless they have made a gradual ascent, visitors to La Paz may experience headaches, sickness, exhaustion, or other symptoms of altitude sickness.

▶ Oncoming traffic beware!—the road to La Paz is high and narrow.

ROADS OF DEATH

Roads through remote mountainous areas provide vital links with the outside world—but often at a terrible cost. Narrow highland routes are notoriously dangerous. They may be made hazardous by snow, ice, mist, or mud. Sections may crumble and tumble or be blocked by rockfalls. Many include steep gradients that test any truck or bus to its mechanical limits.

▲ A farmer works the Longsheng rice terraces, which cling to the mountainside in southern China.

Vertical farming

Who would decide to farm on a steep, rocky mountainside? People on every continent have done just that, whether to grow tea, rice, potatoes, or maize. They have carved out walled terraces and ledges that prevent precious soil from being washed or blown away. They have devised ingenious channels to irrigate the crops, making the maximum possible use of land.

LAVA Lands

Some forces of nature cannot be tamed. A volcano that belches out fire, poisonous gases, and lava has always been a sight to inspire awe and terror in humans. People who make their homes near active volcanoes are perilously close to deadly disaster every day. So why do they do it, and how do they cope?

HALT THE FLOW

Gushing lava can form a sticky wall of black, liquified rock that glows red hot. Parts of this flow can reach speeds of up to 18 mph (30 km/h), but generally it advances much more slowly. Any village that stands in its relentless path is soon engulfed. Engineers try to divert the flow by building walls or creating mounds and ditches with diggers, bulldozers, and explosives.

Sicilian firefighters use hoses to cool a lava flow from Mount Etna while bulldozers shift the solidified mass into banks.

RICH, BLACK EARTH →

Soil created from volcanic rock is often rich in minerals and very fertile. Crops grow well, which is why it is tempting to return to the danger zone. Some volcanoes may not erupt for hundreds of years at a time—so farmers push their luck and work the land while they can. However, there is always a danger that a new eruption may damage their crops.

THE NOTION OF HELL—WIDESPREAD IN MEDIEVAL EUROPE—MAY HAVE DERIVED FROM PEOPLE'S EXPERIENCE OF VOLCANIC CRATERS.

A setback for the farmers—as ash from the Shinmoedake volcano in Japan covers new crops.

A helicopter flies over smoke and ash billowing from the Puehuye-Cordon Calle volcanic chain in Chile.

TELLTALE SIGNS

When will it blow? Volcanic eruptions are very hard to predict, but scientists keep a close watch on high-risk hotspots, via satellites and on the ground. They monitor earthquake activity, deformation of the ground, water courses, and gas emissions. They may even climb down into active craters wearing protective suits. Everything must be done to protect life and property.

YELLOW POISON

Volcanic gases contain large amounts of sulfur. As they cool, this solidifies in the form of bright-yellow crystals. Sulfur is often found in the volcanic "ring of fire" that surrounds the Pacific ocean. People in Java mine the sulfur at the Kawah Ijen volcano. It is used for making chemicals.

Poorly paid miners don't wear masks at Kawah Ijen, so are at risk of inhaling poisonous gases.

The nearby village of San Juan Parangaricutiro was buried by lava from the fast-growing Paricutin volcano. The church tower is all that remains of the old village.

UNDER THE VOLCANO!

One day in 1943 a crack opened up in a field in Mexico, in a village called Paricutin. A new volcano grew up, and in just one year it had grown to 1,102 ft (336 m) high. By 1952, it was 1,391 ft (424 m) high.

The Last Cave DWELLERS

Caves can be dark, damp, echoey places that may be home to thousands of nesting bats or birds. They can be dangerous, too—rock falls may block entrances and rising water can flood lower levels. Despite this, from earliest times humans have sought shelter and refuge in caves and even made them their homes. In some parts of the world today, people still do...

Rooms in the rocks

Zhongdong means "the middle cave"—and that's just what it is: one of three big holes, and the best one for living in. The limestone cave, one of many in southwest China, is home to 18 families of the Miao people, who live in this region. Each family has its own area with walls made of bamboo matting. Wood is used for cooking and heating. Originally life in the cave was extremely tough, but now th cave has lighting, television, and household appliances.

▼ Rice is served up from the cooking pot in one of the cave's kitchens.

Home farm

The people of Zhongdong grow maize outside in the sunlight and also raise animals to sell. Even their livestock pens are located in the cave. Other food and general supplies must be carried along the track, up the mountainside. It's hard work!

◄ A cow is led out of the cave into the daylight. As well as cattle, the people of Zhongdong raise goats, pigs, and chickens.

ZHONGDONG COVERS ABOUT 290,600 SQ FT (27,000 SQ M) AND HAS A ROOF OF 165 FT (50 M)—IT IS THE SIZE OF A BIG AIRCRAFT HANGAR.

Cave school

The cave also houses a school, which serves a very wide area. Some children walk for hours over the mountains to reach the school. Others stay in the cave as boarders. There are six classes numbering about 180 pupils in total, and eight or so teachers. The cave has its own playground, and older children like to play basketball there. There are also evening classes for adults.

▼ Young children attend class at Zhongdong, probably the only cave school in the world.

▶ A man stands at the entrance to his cave home. None of the "houses" have roofs—the cave's roof provides shelter.

NATURAL WATER

The Zhongdong cave was originally shaped and eroded by the force of water, and its people used to collect bucketfuls of water from the drips and trickles seeping through crevices in the porous rocks. That did not provide enough for their needs during the dry season, so they built concrete reservoirs to conserve the supply.

LAKESIDE Living

Lakes have always provided humans with the essentials of life—from fresh water for fishing and waterfowl for eating. However, living beside a lake has its dangers. After heavy rains, water may flood surrounding villages. Lakes may become silted up or blocked with vegetation. Some lakes have turned out to threaten life itself.

▲ The floating islands of the Uros, all made from totora reed.

Reeds for survival

Lake Titicaca lies on the border between Bolivia and Peru, high in the Andes mountains. A type of reed called totora grows there. The local Uros people used it to create 44 floating islands in the lake, and to build their homes and boats. Long ago, living on the islands protected the Uros from enemy attack.

▲ A fisherman on Er Lake in southwest China works with cormorants to bring in the catch.

EXPLODING LAKES

"Exploding lakes" in Cameroon contain carbon dioxide or methane under high pressure. Volcanic activity, earthquakes, or storms can all trigger a massive gas leak. In 1984, 37 people choked to death when toxic gases erupted from the depths of Lake Monoun. Two years later over 1,700 people died beside Lake Nyos. Installing a fountain to disperse the gases can prevent a deadly buildup.

▶ Scientists collect samples from the gaseous carbon dioxide fountain.

Fishing with cormorants

In China and Japan, villagers living by lakes and rivers have used cormorants to catch fish for 1,000 years or more. A neck ring prevents the birds from swallowing the larger fish, but they are rewarded with smaller tidbits. Today there may be easier ways to catch fish, but few easier ways to attract tourists!

1973

2009

VANISHING WATER

The Aral Sea in Central Asia was once one of the four biggest lakes in the world. Over 50 years, it shrank to one tenth of its original size, breaking up into small bodies of water. Too much water was being channeled off to irrigate distant cotton fields. This spelled the end for the fishing and shipping industries. There was widespread economic hardship. Lack of moisture turned the landscape into desert, with rusting ships left high and dry.

◄ Going, going, almost gone—greedy use of a fragile resource proved to be a disaster for the Aral Sea.

► An Intha woman uses a boat to reach the gardens and pick her crop of tomatoes.

Floating gardens

Some 70,000 Intha people live around the shallow waters of Inle Lake, in Burma (Myanmar). They catch fish and grow fruit and vegetables in floating gardens in the lake. These gardens are made from a compost of water weed, anchored by bamboo poles. The lake provides rich nutrients and the gardens rise and fall with the water level, avoiding the risk of flooding in the rainy season.

Rivers bring water for drinking, and their fertile mud is a bonus for farmers along the banks. River power can be harnessed for watermills and hydroelectric turbines. However, rivers can be a curse as well as a blessing. If they change course, towns may be stranded. If they become raging torrents, floodwater can devastate properties—and lives.

DANGERS LURK, HAZARDS ABOUND. THE RIVER RAGES ON. CAN YOU SURVIVE?

RIVER RAGE

PADDLE YOUR OWN CANOE

In remote areas, rivers offer transport routes that are vital for trade, transport, and fishing. In Papua New Guinea, villagers living by rivers still use axes or fire to hollow out tree trunks and make them into dugout canoes.

▼ The Asmat people of West Papua use their woodworking skills to make canoes.

AT TIMES 75 PERCENT OF BANGLADESH HAS BEEN UNDER WATER.

Ready for the floods. Inundation can destroy crops, cause disease, and disrupt transport.

Modern dams have saved many lives, but also created some environmental problems.

Cherrapunji is one of the wettest spots on Earth. Root bridges cross its many waterways.

GREEN BRIDGES

The forests of Meghalaya in northeast India are crisscrossed with streams and rivers. The local Khasi people create bridges by training Bengal fig trees to grow along bamboo poles placed across rivers. Within 10 or 15 years the trees' tangled roots have formed strong bridges across the water, and handrails and paving stones can be added.

CHINA'S SORROW

"China's Sorrow" is another name for the Huang He River, in northern China. This river carries a fine yellow mud, and silting up has made it change course many times. Its floods have killed millions of people. Attempts to protect the land with levees have hindered natural drainage.

HIGH AND DRY

Houses in Old Dhaka are built on stilts, to allow for seasonal flooding. Rivers fan out across Bangladesh to form the Ganges delta, carrying meltwater from the Himalayas. Loss of vegetation and erosion upstream have increased the flooding, made worse by monsoon rains.

SWAMPED
Out

Squelching mud, murky water, rotting vegetation, insects that sting, and reptiles that bite—marshes and swamps hardly make an ideal home. Yet against the odds, humans have settled in some of the world's most treacherous wetlands.

▲ The Marsh Arabs' way of life has survived despite disruption by warfare and drainage of many marshes.

Miracle of the marshes

Floating villages built of reeds can be seen in the southeast of Iraq, where the Tigris and Euphrates rivers spill into a maze of reedbeds, waterways, and wetlands. This region is home to the Madan or Marsh Arabs. A combination of agriculture and years of warfare have displaced many Marsh Arabs from their homelands. Large areas of marshland have been drained and lost forever. However, water is now flowing back to some areas.

Super dung

In some areas of the Sudd— a vast swamp in South Sudan— floods recede during the dry season to reveal grassy pastures, which are grazed by cattle. The Dinka, Nuer, and Shilluk peoples burn fires of cattle dung and smear the white ash on themselves and their precious cattle. This acts as an insect repellent. It is effective in keeping away the clouds of flies, which can spread disease.

◄ Ash gives this Dinka herder—and his cattle—a ghostly appearance.

THE AVERAGE AREA OF THE SUDD IS 11,500 SQ MI (30,000 SQ KM). WHEN THE NILE FLOODS THIS RISES TO 50,200 SQ MI (130,000 SQ KM).

Deadly insects

Warm, stagnant water in tropical swamps is a breeding ground for insects and small mollusks that pass on diseases. When some species of female mosquito feed on human blood, they pass on the malaria parasite. Malaria kills about 1.2 million people worldwide each year. Protection includes vaccination, medication, window and door screens, mosquito nets, and the draining of swamps that harbor mosquito larvae.

▼ Aircraft release chemicals over swamps in Florida, U.S., to eradicate mosquito larvae.

▼ Being a floating fisherman has its drawbacks—there is a risk of being attacked by hippos or crocodiles.

Fishers of the Sudd

In South Sudan, the White Nile overflows across the plains, forming the Sudd wetlands. Traveling through the channels in a steamer can take days, even weeks. Water hyacinth and papyrus stretch to the horizon, and all sense of time and direction can be lost. Peoples of the Sudd fish from small wooden canoes. They build makeshift camps on the dense mats of floating vegetation and dry their catch in the sun.

ALLIGATORS AS NEIGHBORS

If you live in the wetlands of Florida or Louisiana, U.S., you share your home with giant reptiles. A male alligator is king of the swamps, growing to more than 13 ft (4 m) in length. Alligators are dangerous, but humans are more so—widespread hunting left this species on the brink of extinction in the 1950s. Hunting is now controlled and many 'gators are farmed for their leathery hide.

▶ Research has shown that alligators do us a favor, by killing off pests—and attracting tourism.

ISLAND
Challenges

Even some of the most remote islands on our planet have been settled on by people over the ages. Some islands were reached after migration or exploration across vast oceans. Others were discovered by shipwreck or other accident. Islands can offer a paradise to those who live there, but they can also be hard to reach, or have scant resources for survival.

Sea level city

▼ If sea levels rise, Malé could be submerged. If coral reefs die, it would not be shielded from storms.

Malé is a city in the middle of the sparkling blue waters of the Indian Ocean. It is the capital of the Maldives, a nation perched on a long chain of low-lying coral islands. The islanders traditionally depended on fishing for their livelihood, but now tourism is the key to success. However, the whole island is now built up and densely populated. Fresh water is supplied through desalination, an expensive process that removes salt from seawater.

Mangroves for Tuvalu

From October to March each year, storms blow across the Pacific Ocean and batter the tiny islands of Tuvalu, a nation with a population of less than 11,000. The winds bring rain, which is collected in tanks for drinking water. High tides cause flooding, and rising sea levels pose a severe challenge to a sustainable future. The islanders plan to build up the coastal defenses by planting mangrove trees—their dense, tangled roots would collect mud and form a barrier against the ocean waves.

▼ Mangrove seedlings will grow into trees that will protect the island coastlines.

GARBAGE ISLAND

In the Maldives, garbage was once dumped on coral reefs for 20 years, which created a new island. This is now 1.2 mi (2 km) long and parts have been sold off to industry. However, much of the waste was toxic and the burning of waste every day poisoned the atmosphere. The dumping has now stopped, but many fear the damage to the environment is already done.

▼ "Garbage island," known as Thilafushi, was a toxic dumping ground.

Isolated!

Islands in remote places can feel cut off from the wider world. The coral islands of Tokelau, in the middle of the Pacific Ocean, have no airports or harbors. Visitors and supplies are landed by boat. Tokelau is the world's smallest economy, producing coconuts and handicrafts—and stamps for collectors. It is a territory of New Zealand, more than 2,100 mi (3,360 km) away. Many islanders have settled to work there and send money home.

▼ Unloading supplies on Nukunonu atoll, Tokelau, is a laborious process.

TRISTAN DA CUNHA, IN THE SOUTH ATLANTIC OCEAN, IS THE WORLD'S MOST REMOTE ARCHIPELAGO. IT IS 1,750 MI (2,816 KM) FROM SOUTH AFRICA AND 2,090 MI (3,360 KM) FROM SOUTH AMERICA.

Fishing frenzy

Island coasts around the world offer an obvious food source for local people—fish and other seafood. These Fijians from Vatulele island are fishing by a method called *yavirau*. When the tide ebbs, a boat crosses the lagoon, laying a long rope made of forest creeper, coconut fronds, and leaves. A big circle of people wade into the shallows and walk shoreward with the rope, creating an ever smaller circle in which the fish are trapped.

▲ The big fish roundup of *yavirau* involves the whole community.

OCEAN
Living

The power of the ocean should never be underestimated. Strong currents can drag swimmers out to sea, waves can pound cliffs to rubble, and even the biggest ships are at the mercy of ocean storms. Even so, humans venture fearlessly into the marine environment, to explore and to make their living.

Outrigger!

A sailing canoe is sleek and fast, but in rough water it becomes dangerously unstable. The solution, developed over the ages, was to fix an extension float or floats parallel to the hull. This is called an outrigger. Outrigger canoes may still be seen across the Indian and Pacific oceans, from Sri Lanka to the Hawaiian islands.

▶ Outriggers made possible the biggest marine migrations in history, undertaken by Polynesian seafarers between 1500 BC and AD 1000.

Gypsies of the sea

Several peoples of southeast Asia, such as the Bajau, Chao Ley, Moken, and Uruk Lawoi, are known as "Sea Gypsies." Originally, these families would spend their whole lives wandering the ocean on small wooden boats, living by fishing or diving. Today, many of them have settled in one place, sometimes earning more money from tourism than fishing. However, many are still seafarers. It was said they alone anticipated the tsunami that devastated the region in 2004.

▶ Sea Gypsies built a fishing village on Panyi island, in Thailand. It is now a popular tourist destination.

SHELLS AND STICKS

How to navigate the oceans? At first glance this framework of sticks and cowrie shells looks like a random pattern. In reality it is a traditional chart, used by the Marshall Islanders of the Pacific to map the position of islands (shells) and ocean currents (sticks).

PERCHED IN THE OCEAN
Line fishing from the shore is easy if you have rocks or jetties in the right place. These fishermen from Sri Lanka have found another solution to improve their access to the sea. They drive a 13-ft- (4-m-) long wooden pole into the coral reef. They climb up onto a small crossbar called a *petta*, and there they perch for hours on end. They catch small fish, storing them in plastic bags until it's time to go home and cook the next meal.

MANY SEAWEEDS ARE SURVIVAL SUPERFOODS, RICH IN CALCIUM, IODINE, IRON, AND MAGNESIUM.

▶ Don't fall asleep on the job! Fishermen on sticks bring in the mackerel around Kathaluwa in Sri Lanka.

Deep-sea vision
The Moken are marine nomads who live in Burma (Myanmar) and Thailand. They are phenomenal freedivers from an early age, collecting sea cucumbers from the ocean floor and fishing with nets and spears. Scientific research has shown that their eyes have developed the ability to focus underwater far better than most other people.

▲ A man fishes using compressed air supplied from the surface through a tube—a very risky way to make a living.

TRAPPED!

PAULA LOPEZ Copiapó, Chile   LIVE

Our search for minerals and fuel has taken miners deep underground, into dark, hot, perilous environments. Mining shafts may collapse or become blocked by rock falls or floods. Poisonous gases may fill the workings, and one tiny spark set off an explosion. Miners and rescuers need to be resourceful and brave. Few were more so than these Chileans, trapped underground on August 5, 2010.

ROCKFALL

BREAKTHROUGH

Day 1: Reports come in of a rock fall at the San José copper and gold mine, near Copiapó—33 miners are trapped 3 mi (5 km) from the mine entrance, 2,300 ft (700 m) underground.

Day 3: Plans are being made to reach the miners through a ventilation shaft when more cave-ins occur. Rescue teams decide to dig boreholes and send down listening probes. Relatives, crowds, and the press set up a camp at the surface.

Day 69: The first miner is winched to the surface, wearing dark glasses to protect his eyes. He emerges from the capsule. The last miner to come up is shift foreman Luis Urzua. Pictures of the rescue are flashed around the world and seen by about 1,000 million television viewers.

Weeks later: Many of the miners found it difficult to get over their ordeal. They suffered from stress and found it difficult to get work.

RESCUE

Day 17: A drill breaks through to a refuge where the miners had been eating when the cave-in occurred. They attach a note to say that all of them are still alive. A camera is lowered and shows the miners in good condition. Supplies are sent down. The miners organize work shifts and clear rubble. They exercise to keep fit in the available tunnel. They write letters, play games—and sleep.

Day 25: Drilling begins on the first of three rescue shafts, with international and Chilean teams. Naval engineers and NASA design steel rescue capsules.

Day 65: Rescue shaft B is the first to reach the miners.

CONCRETE Jungle

Are cities really a triumph of people over nature? Here are environments expressly designed for humans. The canyons are made of concrete, steel, and glass instead of rock. The winds are funneled around skyscrapers. The temperature can be controlled by air conditioning—but in fact these urban landscapes can be every bit as savage as the natural world.

▶ Chinese cities are among the world's murkiest. On some days only the tops of skyscrapers rise above the haze, shown here in Suzhou, China.

Shanty town

They call them favelas, squatter camps, bidonvilles, shanty towns, or slums. The houses are shacks, assembled from scraps by poor people arriving in the city in search of work. They have no proper drains, no safe electricity supply, a high risk of fire, and no law and order. Sometimes the settlements are bulldozed, but unless the authorities improve social conditions, the misery will not go away.

▲ A tough place to grow up—makeshift homes cover the hillside in Rio de Janeiro, Brazil.

Toxic smog

Smog originally meant a choking mixture of sooty smoke and fog. Today exhaust fumes from cars and chemicals from factories and power plants add to the misery, reacting with sunlight to create a toxic haze. This air pollution can lead to breathing problems and even lung cancer. The solution? Controlling emissions and reducing vehicle use.

A WALK ON THE WILD SIDE

The world's cities are surprisingly friendly places for wildlife, but animals can cause problems. Large flocks of pigeons or starlings can create for wildlife, but animals can cause problems. Food in the inner cities such as bears or foxes. Termites may eat away at woodwork. Even inside the home, life can be made a nightmare by unwelcome guests—rats, cockroaches, ants, termites, houseflies, fleas, and bedbugs. They are more than just a nuisance—they can spread serious disease.

▲ Utter devastation—houses were damaged and five people were killed when violent storms caused tons of garbage to hit a residential area.

▶ Hungry polar bears are a problem in the Canadian town of Churchill, Manitoba. They hunt for food and may attack people. Persistent raiders may need to be airlifted out of town!

AN AVALANCHE OF GARBAGE

The forces of nature can devastate a city. Blizzards and floods can bring cities to a halt. Heatwaves can cause widespread loss of life. In 2011 a tropical storm, or typhoon, in the Philippines destroyed the retaining wall of a refuse tip in the northern city of Baguio. Garbage poured down the hillside, engulfing houses and people.

Up on the roof

Cities are short of space for gardens. Sometimes there are vegetable plots called allotments, where city dwellers can grow food for the table. In many cities, from New York to Singapore, gardens are also springing up on city center rooftops, which can provide vegetables directly. This also adds a layer of insulation, reducing heat loss from the buildings.

▶ Bringing in an urban harvest. This rooftop in eastern China has been converted into a working farm.

Wish You Were Here?

Humans are intelligent creatures—sometimes too clever for their own good. Among the most hostile places on Earth are natural landscapes devastated by weapons and warfare, environmental disasters, industrial accidents, and pollution. Cleaning up the mess and making it safe pose a challenge for the future.

The islands of Bikini Atoll in the Pacific Ocean were known for their tranquility and beauty—until 1946. Inhabitants were evacuated to other islands and, over a 12-year period, 23 U.S. nuclear bombs were exploded on the site, as part of a weapons testing program. Although radiation levels have fallen, it is still not safe for people to live there permanently or eat food grown there.

Bikini Atoll

A 150-megaton hydrogen bomb blasts Bikini Atoll on March 1, 1954.

Chernobyl

In 1986 there was an explosion and fire at the Chernobyl nuclear power plant, near Pripyat, in what is now the Ukraine. Radioactive particles spread over much of Europe. The number of deaths is disputed, but there is an ongoing legacy of cancer and deformity in the region. Hundreds of thousands of workers were needed to shut down the plant, at the cost of billions of dollars.

An exclusion zone of 1,000 sq mi (2,600 sq km) still surrounds Pripyat. Streets are deserted and buildings are abandoned.

Black smoke billows over the Gulf during a controlled burn off of the leaking oil.

Deepwater Horizon

In 2010 Deepwater Horizon, a rig boring the deepest ever offshore oil well, exploded, caught fire, and sank off the coast of Texas, U.S. Mud, gas, and black oil belched out into the sea, unchecked for 87 days. Eleven crew members were killed, and the economy of the Gulf Coast was devastated. Fishing boats, no longer able to operate, were called in to help with the cleanup. Nearly 5 million barrels of oil leaked into the Gulf, to be dispersed with yet more poisonous chemicals.

Yamuna River

The Yamuna River carries meltwater from the glaciers of the Himalayas all the way to India's plains. Once its waters were clear and sparkling, but today the Yamuna carries pesticides, fertilizers, and weedkillers, washed from the lands it passes through. It is filled with toxic industrial waste from more than 500 factories, and vast amounts of garbage and sewage from the capital, New Delhi.

Deadly minefields

Landmines are bombs buried in the ground. They explode if a person or vehicle passes by, but remain a threat to innocent life long after wars have ended. In 1997 many countries agreed to ban landmines, but today perhaps 100 million devices are still buried, killing a person somewhere in the world every 22 minutes. Landmine clearance endangers lives, but new robots have been developed with remote control capabilities.

The Taj Mahal rises majestically in the distance, beyond the garbage-strewn banks of the Yamuna River.

In southern Tanzania, a rat is trained to sniff out antitank landmines.

Brutal BATTLES

Discover the facts behind battles that have become legend. From supreme bravery to extreme brutality—this is the no-holds-barred account.

◀ Plate armor was not easily penetrated by even the strongest swords, so combatants aimed for any weak points, or delivered blows with crushing weapons, such as maces.

CHARIOT Warfare

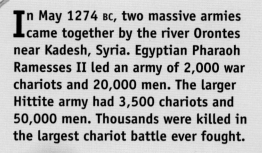

In May 1274 BC, two massive armies came together by the river Orontes near Kadesh, Syria. Egyptian Pharaoh Ramesses II led an army of 2,000 war chariots and 20,000 men. The larger Hittite army had 3,500 chariots and 50,000 men. Thousands were killed in the largest chariot battle ever fought.

RAMESSES II

One of the most important pharaohs of ancient Egypt, Ramesses II (1303–1213 BC) became king in 1279 BC, aged 25, and ruled for 66 years. He waged war against the Hittites to the north and the Libyans to the west. In paintings and carvings, he was often shown leading his troops into battle on his war chariot. Among the many temples he built were two vast constructions carved out of the solid rock at Abu Simbel by the river Nile.

Battle by the river

Ramesses II and the lead division of the Egyptian army advanced north toward Kadesh. They thought the Hittites were further north and set up camp. The Hittites, however, were hidden on the other side of the river Orontes—where they launched a surprise ambush on the rest of the Egyptian army, before attacking the camp. As more Hittite chariots crossed the river, Ramesses II mounted a counterattack. The battle swung to and fro until both sides withdrew. Many of the Hittites drowned in the river Orontes as they fled.

▲ At the Battle of Kadesh, Ramesses II drove his chariot into battle. Normally he would have had a driver in the chariot with him.

EGYPTIANS VS. HITTITES

◄ The peace treaty has been preserved on stone tablets.

Time for peace

After the battle was over, Ramesses II declared he had won a great victory. However, neither side had won. The Hittites occupied two northern Egyptian provinces in Lebanon while Ramesses returned to Egypt. In 1258, Ramesses signed a peace treaty with the Hittite king Hattusili III to end the war. This was the first time in history that such a treaty had been signed between two former enemies.

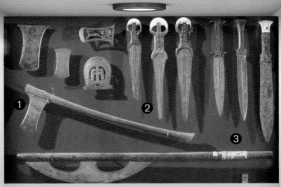

EGYPTIAN WEAPONS
❶ Battle ax ❷ Daggers with ivory handles ❸ Epsilon-shaped ax

Attack and defense

The main weapon of the Egyptians was a wooden bow, strengthened with horn. Its wooden arrows had tips of bronze, iron, or bone and could be fired to a distance of 575 ft (175 m). Soldiers on both sides also fought with axes, long and short swords, and bronze hatchets. They protected themselves with simple bronze shields.

WHEELED WAR VEHICLES

Drawn by two horses, the lightweight wooden chariot had two widely spaced, six-spoked wheels and a platform for the crew to stand on—one to steer and the other to fight. A well-driven chariot could reach a speed of up to 24 mph (38 km/h) and turn sharp corners with ease.

Battle of
MARATHON

In 490 BC, King Darius I, leader of the powerful Persian Empire, decided to crush his rebellious Greek subjects. He assembled a massive force of about 25,000 men. They set sail across the Aegean Sea in a fleet of 600 triremes—large ships powered by three banks of oars. The battle that took place at Marathon ended Darius' dreams—the Greek troops overwhelmed the larger Persian army.

The attack

The Persian fleet landed at Marathon, close to their main target of Athens. Its force of 25,000 men outnumbered the Greeks two to one. Greek commander Miltiades arranged his hoplites into a long, thin phalanx that advanced at the enemy. The Greeks overwhelmed the Persian flanks, or ends. Greek troops in the center, however, came under Persian arrow fire and began to crumble. Seeing they were in trouble, more Greeks rushed in, causing the Persian force to collapse and retreat.

▼ The close formation of the Greek soldiers enabled them to swamp the Persians, leading to a decisive victory.

▼ In the phalanx formation, enemy soldiers could not get past the line of shields.

The ultimate formation

Greek soldiers were called hoplites. They went into battle armed with a long spear, a sword, and a large, round bronze shield. They wore bronze helmets, linen cuirasses (body armor), and greaves (shin guards). In battle, hoplites formed a tight-knit phalanx with their shields locked together around them and their spears raised.

Escape by sea

By the end of the battle, the Persians had lost 6,400 men, the Greeks only 192. In a disorganized fashion, the remaining Persian army fled the battlefield, pursued by the Greeks. Some drowned in nearby swamps when trying to reach their large warships.

▶ About two thirds of the Persian army managed to board their ships and sail home to Asia.

ANCIENT GREEK SOLDIERS RARELY RODE HORSES BECAUSE IF THEY HURLED A SPEAR, THEY WERE LIKELY TO FALL OFF BACKWARD!

The news runner

Greek legend states that after the Battle of Marathon, a messenger called Pheidippedes, who had just fought in the battle, ran home to Athens to announce the victory. He ran 26 mi (42 km) without stopping, bursting into the Athens assembly to announce, "We won." He then died. The modern-day marathon race commemorates Pheidippedes' achievement.

◀ A statue of Pheidippedes stands along the Olympic marathon route, near Athens.

CONQUERING
the World

▲ Alexander leads his Macedonian cavalry over the river Granicus before attacking the Persians on the other bank.

Few people in history earn the title of "the Great," but one such man was Alexander. Aged 20, Alexander became king of Macedonia. He won three major victories to conquer the vast Persian Empire. He intended to invade India and the rest of the known world, but his troops wanted to return home to Macedonia. His dream of world domination did not come true.

GRANICUS, 334 BC

Alexander and his army of 43,000 infantry (foot soldiers) and 6,100 cavalry (horsemen) crossed the waterway that separated Greece from the Persian Empire in Asia. They crossed the river far from the main Persian army, only encountering a smaller Persian force by the river Granicus, outside Troy. The Persians had to quickly rearrange their troops, allowing Alexander's army to overwhelm them.

> ALEXANDER THE GREAT AND HIS ARMY MARCHED NEARLY 20,000 MI (32,000 KM) OVER THE COURSE OF HIS 11-YEAR CAMPAIGN.

ISSUS, 334 BC

After his victory at Granicus, Alexander moved south, freeing cities from Persian rule. A far larger Persian force, commanded by King Darius III, intercepted the Macedonian army at Issus, in what is now Turkey. Although the Macedonians were heavily outnumbered, they were stronger, well-trained soldiers. Darius abandoned the battle, leaving behind his mother, wife, two daughters, and large amounts of treasure.

▲ A Roman mosaic showing the Battle of Issus. Alexander (left) spears a Persian horseman as King Darius of Persia (far right) escapes on his chariot.

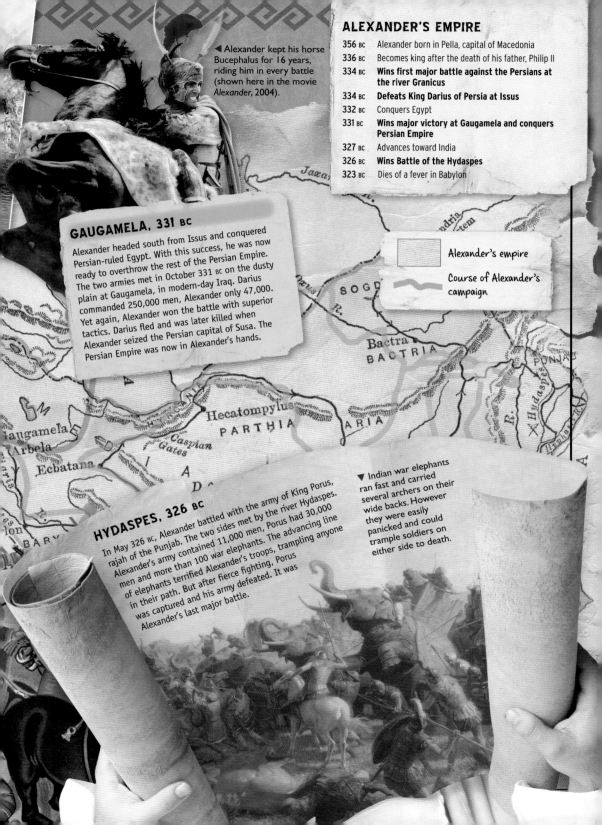

◄ Alexander kept his horse Bucephalus for 16 years, riding him in every battle (shown here in the movie *Alexander*, 2004).

ALEXANDER'S EMPIRE

356 BC	Alexander born in Pella, capital of Macedonia
336 BC	Becomes king after the death of his father, Philip II
334 BC	**Wins first major battle against the Persians at the river Granicus**
334 BC	**Defeats King Darius of Persia at Issus**
332 BC	Conquers Egypt
331 BC	**Wins major victory at Gaugamela and conquers Persian Empire**
327 BC	Advances toward India
326 BC	**Wins Battle of the Hydaspes**
323 BC	Dies of a fever in Babylon

☐ Alexander's empire

〜 Course of Alexander's campaign

GAUGAMELA, 331 BC

Alexander headed south from Issus and conquered Persian-ruled Egypt. With this success, he was now ready to overthrow the rest of the Persian Empire. The two armies met in October 331 BC on the dusty plain at Gaugamela, in modern-day Iraq. Darius commanded 250,000 men, Alexander only 47,000. Yet again, Alexander won the battle with superior tactics. Darius fled and was later killed when Alexander seized the Persian capital of Susa. The Persian Empire was now in Alexander's hands.

HYDASPES, 326 BC

In May 326 BC, Alexander battled with the army of King Porus, rajah of the Punjab. The two sides met by the river Hydaspes. Alexander's army contained 11,000 men, Porus had 30,000 men and more than 100 war elephants. The advancing line of elephants terrified Alexander's troops, trampling anyone in their path. But after fierce fighting, Porus was captured and his army defeated. It was Alexander's last major battle.

▼ Indian war elephants ran fast and carried several archers on their wide backs. However they were easily panicked and could trample soldiers on either side to death.

DEADLIEST Days

For more than a century, the empires of Rome and Carthage fought three long and bloody wars—known as the Punic Wars—for control of the Mediterranean Sea. Of all the great battles fought, the Roman defeat at Cannae in 216 BC was one of the deadliest battles of all time.

ROMANS VS. CARTHAGINIANS

264–241 BC	**First Punic War:** Rome and Carthage fight for control of Sicily. Carthage is defeated
260 BC	Roman navy defeats Carthaginians at Mylae
218–201 BC	**Second Punic War:** Carthage fights to avenge defeat in first war, but loses
218 BC	Hannibal inflicts major defeat on the Romans at Trebia
217 BC	Hannibal wins major battle at Lake Trasimene
216 BC	Hannibal inflicts another massive defeat on the Romans at Cannae
149–146 BC	**Third Punic War:** Rome inflicts final defeat of Carthage and razes city to the ground

▼ During the first Punic War, the Roman fleet defeated the Carthaginians at Mylae off the coast of Sicily.

First Punic War 264–241 BC

When Rome went to war with Carthage, Tunisia, in 264 BC to seize Sicily, Italy, its armies soon controlled the island but not the seas. Rome quickly built a fleet of triremes—boats with three tiers of oars—and developed the corvus—a long board with a spike underneath. When an enemy ship came close, the Romans dropped the corvus into its deck, allowing them to board the ship and kill the enemy. This innovation brought them success at Mylae in 260 BC. In 250 BC, the Romans invaded North Africa to end the war but were thrown out. Fighting dragged on until peace was made in 241 BC. Sicily became a Roman province.

▲ In 218 BC, the Carthaginian general Hannibal led 37 elephants and an army of 30,000 men across the Alps to launch a surprise attack on the Romans from the rear.

Second Punic War 218–201 BC

In July 216 BC, the Carthaginians seized a major Roman supply depot at Cannae in southern Italy. A Roman army of 86,000 soldiers set out to defeat them. The two armies met on August 2. The Roman lines pushed forward, but were attacked from the rear by Hannibal's horsemen. The result was a massacre. More than 50,000 Roman soldiers were killed.

BEASTLY PROTECTION

The Carthaginians wore elaborate breastplates and fought with long spears and javelins. They rode elephants in battle, although if panicked, these beasts could flatten their own soldiers. Their Numidian allies from North Africa rode horses without saddles, controlling them with sticks and spoken commands. Celtic allies from France used swords and spears.

THE ROMANS CALLED THE CARTHAGINIANS THE POENI ("PHOENICIANS") AND SO THE THREE WARS BETWEEN THEM BECAME KNOWN AS THE PUNIC WARS.

Third Punic War 149–146 BC

Carthage was heavily defeated in the Second Punic War. However, many Romans still considered Carthage to be a threat. In 149 BC, Rome sent a large army to lay siege to Carthage. The siege went on for three years until starvation and disease weakened resistance. In spring 146 BC, the Romans broke through the city walls. All 50,000 inhabitants surrendered.

▲ When seizing Carthage, the Romans demolished every building and sent its people into slavery.

Hilltop SIEGE

High above the Dead Sea in Israel lies the hilltop fortress of Masada. In AD 72, 960 Jewish rebels, who were fighting the Roman occupiers of their country, retreated to this bleak place. The Roman army of 15,000 men laid siege to the fortress for five months. When the Romans finally broke in on April 16, AD 73, they were met with a terrible sight.

THE TARGET—MASADA

The fortress of Masada stood on a rocky hilltop 1,300 ft (400 m) above the Dead Sea. A long wall with many towers surrounded the fortress. Inside were a palace, barracks, armory, and many storehouses. Tanks collected rainwater for drinking. The only access to the fortress was by three narrow paths that led up to fortified gates.

▼ The Masada fortress ruins and surrounding siegeworks are now a UNESCO site.

Northern Palace

Storehouses

Watch Tower

WHEN UNDER ATTACK, GROUPS OF SOLDIERS HELD SHIELDS AROUND THEM TO FORM A TESTUDO (TORTOISE).

BOUDICCA'S REVOLT

The Roman Empire faced many uprisings during its lifetime. Shortly before the Jewish Revolt in AD 73, the Iceni tribe, led by Queen Boudicca, took London and other cities. In a major battle in AD 60, the Romans massacred tens of thousands of Iceni. Boudicca died, probably by taking poison.

▶ A statue of Boudicca and her daughters stands by the river Thames in London, U.K.

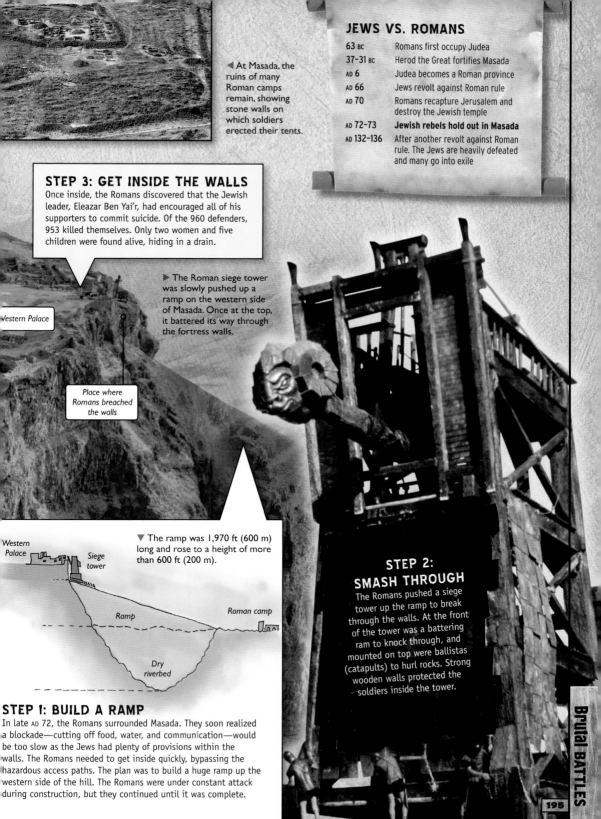

At Masada, the ruins of many Roman camps remain, showing stone walls on which soldiers erected their tents.

STEP 3: GET INSIDE THE WALLS

Once inside, the Romans discovered that the Jewish leader, Eleazar Ben Yai'r, had encouraged all of his supporters to commit suicide. Of the 960 defenders, 953 killed themselves. Only two women and five children were found alive, hiding in a drain.

▶ The Roman siege tower was slowly pushed up a ramp on the western side of Masada. Once at the top, it battered its way through the fortress walls.

Western Palace

Place where Romans breached the walls

Western Palace | Siege tower

▼ The ramp was 1,970 ft (600 m) long and rose to a height of more than 600 ft (200 m).

Ramp

Roman camp

Dry riverbed

STEP 1: BUILD A RAMP

In late AD 72, the Romans surrounded Masada. They soon realized a blockade—cutting off food, water, and communication—would be too slow as the Jews had plenty of provisions within the walls. The Romans needed to get inside quickly, bypassing the hazardous access paths. The plan was to build a huge ramp up the western side of the hill. The Romans were under constant attack during construction, but they continued until it was complete.

STEP 2: SMASH THROUGH

The Romans pushed a siege tower up the ramp to break through the walls. At the front of the tower was a battering ram to knock through, and mounted on top were ballistas (catapults) to hurl rocks. Strong wooden walls protected the soldiers inside the tower.

Brutal BATTLES

195

Death from the Sea

From 793 onward, the Anglo-Saxons of England faced a new threat from the sea. Viking invaders swept up to the coast in their longboats, killing and plundering everywhere they landed. The Anglo-Saxon defenders were brave, but the Vikings more cunning, and battles often led to masses of Anglo-Saxon deaths. Although the Anglo-Saxons formed a number of small kingdoms, their warriors were rarely a match for the ferocious Vikings.

▲ The prow of a longboat was carved with a dragon or beast to strike fear into Viking enemies.

Fearsome longships

Viking raiders traveled the seas in wooden longships. These vessels were up to 71 ft (22 m) long and 16 ft (5 m) wide, and carried a crew of up to 30 warriors. The ships had shallow hulls, so they could sail inland up rivers. In a raid, the Vikings could drag the ships onto a beach—and escape quickly afterward!

The Battle of Maldon

In August 991, a Viking invasion fleet sailed to Essex in eastern England, landing on Northey Island. When the tide was out, the Vikings made their way along the causeway to the mainland, but found their passage blocked by an Anglo-Saxon force of 3,000 men. Viking king Olaf Tryggvason asked that his men be allowed to pass and Anglo-Saxon leader Byrhtnoth agreed. Once on land, the Vikings turned on their enemies and killed them all in battle.

▼ Viking cunning won the day at Maldon, tricking the Anglo-Saxons into a battle they could not win.

Fierce warriors

Viking raiders leapt from their longboats to bring terror to those they attacked. They raided for booty and treasure, but also looked for land to settle on and countries to rule. They valued glory more than life. Before battle, berserker warriors dressed in animal skins and worked themselves up by shouting and biting their shields. They charged at the enemy, howling like wild animals.

Slice and slash

The main Viking weapons were axes, swords, and spears, all made of iron. Long, double-edged swords were used to deliver slashing blows rather than for stabbing the enemy. Horsemen thrust long-handled spears through walls of shields. Spears, arrows, and axes were all thrown at an enemy during a battle. Round shields protected the warriors during combat.

▶ Battleaxes had iron blades up to 12 in (30 cm) across and wooden shafts up to 6.5 ft (2 m) long.

Mass Murder

The Mongols were brutal warriors, killing every enemy they met. Winning battle after battle, they eventually carved out a massive empire that stretched from China in the east across Asia to the Black Sea in the west. In 1258, Mongol armies led by Hulagu captured Baghdad. The city was about to be slaughtered.

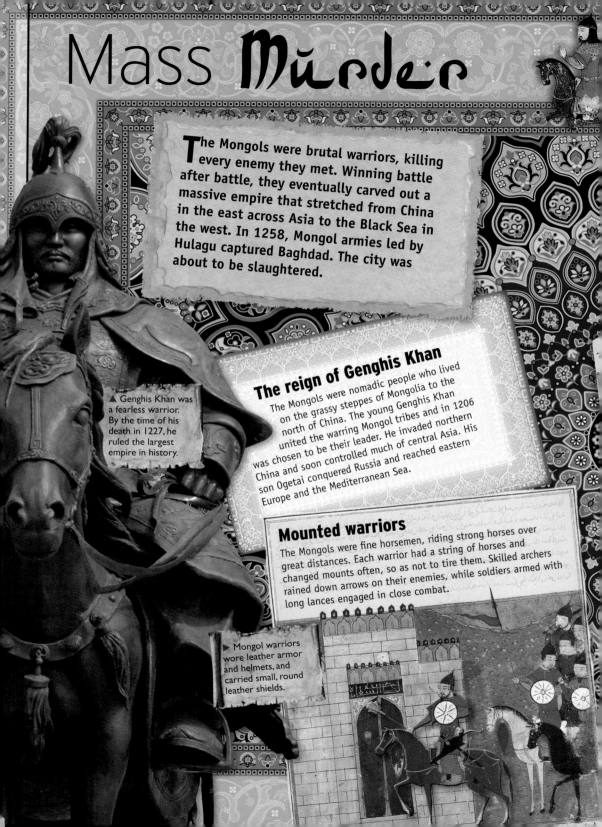

▲ Genghis Khan was a fearless warrior. By the time of his death in 1227, he ruled the largest empire in history.

The reign of Genghis Khan

The Mongols were nomadic people who lived on the grassy steppes of Mongolia to the north of China. The young Genghis Khan united the warring Mongol tribes and in 1206 was chosen to be their leader. He invaded northern China and soon controlled much of central Asia. His son Ogetai conquered Russia and reached eastern Europe and the Mediterranean Sea.

Mounted warriors

The Mongols were fine horsemen, riding strong horses over great distances. Each warrior had a string of horses and changed mounts often, so as not to tire them. Skilled archers rained down arrows on their enemies, while soldiers armed with long lances engaged in close combat.

▶ Mongol warriors wore leather armor and helmets, and carried small, round leather shields.

THE MONGOL EMPIRE

1206	Genghis Khan unites Mongol tribes under his leadership
1211	Genghis Khan invades northern China
1219	Mongols conquer central Asia
1237	Mongols invade Russia
1241	Mongols invade eastern Europe and defeat major German army in Poland
1258	**Led by Hulagu, the Mongols seize Baghdad**
1259	Mongol Empire breaks into separate states
1268-79	Mongols under Kublai Khan conquer southern China

Taking on Baghdad

In 1256, Hulagu—the grandson of Genghis Khan—led his Mongol forces toward Baghdad. The caliph refused to accept Mongol rule and closed the city's gates. Meanwhile, another Mongol force lured a Muslim division onto marshy ground, breached the dykes of the river Euphrates, and drowned them all.

▲ Hulagu ruled the Mongols from 1256 until his death in 1265. During his reign, his armies captured Baghdad and much of the Middle East.

The deadly siege

Hulagu surrounded Baghdad and in February 1258, the Mongol army broke in. They forced the caliph to surrender and massacred all 90,000 inhabitants. The caliph was spared until he revealed where the treasury was hidden. He was then rolled up in a carpet and trampled to death.

▲ The Mongols besieged the city, and once inside the walls, they burned the buildings to the ground.

▲ Although outnumbered, the Minamoto army ambushed the Taira clan and won the Battle of Kurikara.

Sly Samurai

Samurai—the name that brought terror to their enemies. These skilled Japanese warriors fought and died for their masters. Riding into battle on horses, they often dismounted to engage in brutal one-on-one combat, fighting to the death. The winner cut off his opponent's head as proof of his courage and skill.

War at Kurikara

In 1183, a vast Taira army of 100,000 men advanced north to meet the rival Minamoto clan, half its size, at Kurikara. They took up position at the top of a mountain pass and carried out a lengthy archery duel with the Minamoto army in the valley below. While this went on, Minamoto soldiers crept round the enemy's rear and sent a herd of oxen with burning torches tied to their horns up the pass toward the Taira army. The Taira fled in panic, many falling to their deaths from the mountain paths. The rest were massacred. The victorious Minamoto could now take over Japan.

Battle warriors

Samurai were an elite warrior class with a strong code of honor known as *bushido*, which told them how to behave in life. Battle would often start after an argument between rival clans. When the two sides faced each other on a battlefield, the armies followed a strict sequence of events. First, champions from each side rode out to meet each other. The two men would fight on horseback, then take part in hand-to-hand combat. After the duel, fighting broke out between the whole army.

◄ In single combat, samurai fought with swords that had long, curved blades.

MINAMOTO VS. TAIRA

Blades of steel

Swords were the main weapons used by the samurai. The main fighting sword was called a *katana*. It had a long, curving blade, and was held with the sharp edge upward to deliver a swift cut into the enemy. The blades were skilfully crafted out of steel to make them sharp and strong. Samurai also carried a short sword, called a *tanto*, as well as knives and daggers. Strong padded armor protected their bodies from attack.

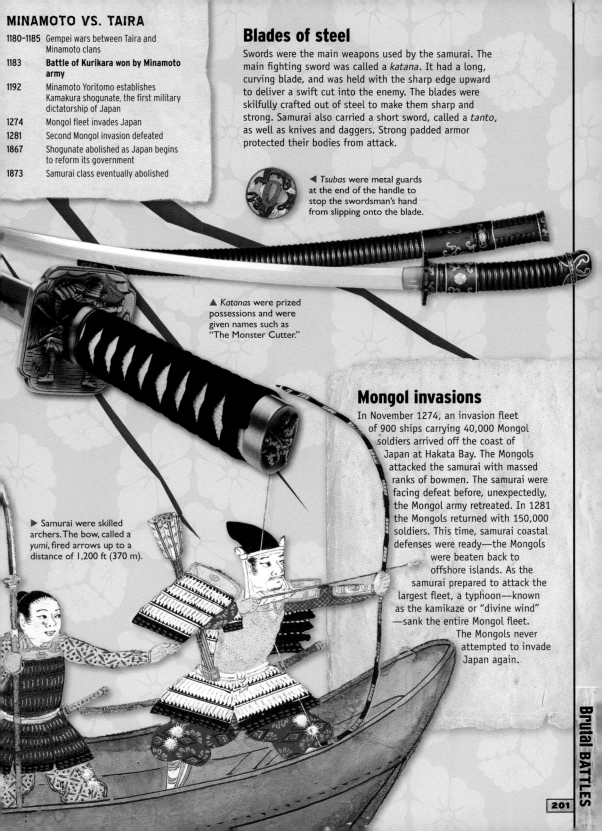

◀ *Tsubas* were metal guards at the end of the handle to stop the swordsman's hand from slipping onto the blade.

▲ *Katanas* were prized possessions and were given names such as "The Monster Cutter."

Mongol invasions

In November 1274, an invasion fleet of 900 ships carrying 40,000 Mongol soldiers arrived off the coast of Japan at Hakata Bay. The Mongols attacked the samurai with massed ranks of bowmen. The samurai were facing defeat before, unexpectedly, the Mongol army retreated. In 1281 the Mongols returned with 150,000 soldiers. This time, samurai coastal defenses were ready—the Mongols were beaten back to offshore islands. As the samurai prepared to attack the largest fleet, a typhoon—known as the kamikaze or "divine wind" —sank the entire Mongol fleet. The Mongols never attempted to invade Japan again.

▶ Samurai were skilled archers. The bow, called a *yumi*, fired arrows up to a distance of 1,200 ft (370 m).

100 Years of War

The longest war in history—known as the Hundred Years War—began in 1337 and ended in 1453, a total of 116 years. The war began when the French claimed the English throne. After many bloody battles, the English were thrown out of France, and ended when Edward III of England were war ended out of France.

Crécy, 1346

The first major battle of the war took place near Crécy, northern France. The small English army took up position on a slope. When the much larger French army arrived, they were tired and wet after a long march. Facing the sun, the French crossbowmen fired first—but their bolts fell short and they were quickly cut down by English arrows. Next, the French knights charged at the English, but the defense was too strong and the French soldiers fell. At least 4,000 Frenchmen were killed, but only 200 English.

▲ The French used crossbows—deadly but slow to load and fire. The English used longbows—

Poitiers, 1356

The second English victory came in 1356 at Poitiers, western France. The English took up position behind a large hedge with a narrow gap through which only four knights could ride abreast. Wave after wave of French knights rode toward the gap, only for their horses to be shot down by the English archers. Finally, the English army charged at the French and attacked them from the rear.

▲ King John II of France surrendered to Edward the Black Prince, commander of the English army, at Poitiers.

Agincourt, 1415

After a long pause, Henry V of England renewed his claim to the French throne and sailed for France. An exhausted 6,000-strong English army faced a French army of 20,000 men. The English planted themselves in woodland by a narrow road. As the French horsemen and foot soldiers became bogged down in muddy ground, the English attacked, clearing the field—another victory. More than 5,000 French soldiers died, with only 300 English deaths.

▲ At the start of the Battle of Agincourt, Henry V of England and his army prayed for victory.

Steel protection

Knights had the best arms and armor and were the most experienced, skilled fighters in an army. Early knights wore chainmail armor, but enemies soon learned how to deliver piercing blows. During the 14th century, plate armor was developed, which was much more difficult for swords and arrows to penetrate. It was made of sheets of steel shaped to fit the body. The helmet was also made of metal, with a hinged visor that could be lifted up and down. A full suit of armor weighed about 55 lb (25 kg).

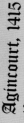

▼ A suit of armor covered the body, arms, and legs. Although heavy, it was flexible enough for the knight to bend and twist.

AGAINST the Odds

The fall of the Inca Empire to the Spanish in 1532 was extraordinary. Armed with guns and horses, which were both unknown to the Incas, less than 200 Spaniards overwhelmed an army of at least 40,000 men and soon captured an empire of 12 million people.

KEEPING RECORDS

The Incas kept detailed records of population, harvests, taxes, and other items. They could not read or write, so instead used a system of knotted, colored strings known as a *quipu* to list everything.

A GREAT EMPIRE

The Inca Empire stretched down the west coast of South America, from what is now Ecuador in the north to Chile in the south. The Incas were great farmers, building terraces along the steep hillsides to plant crops. They connected their long, thin empire together with 12,500 mi (20,100 km) of roads, the greatest road network built since the Roman Empire 1,000 years before.

SOUTH AMERICA

Capturing the empire

In 1532, a long civil war that weakened the Incan Empire ended. Spanish conquistador Pizarro and his 178 men advanced safely inland. On the morning of November 16, Pizarro met the Incan ruler Atahualpa and his 40,000 men at Cajamarca, Peru. The Spanish opened fire and seized Atahualpa. They ransomed him for a room filled with gold, but later killed him. Pizarro then marched on Cuzco, the capital, which he took without a fight.

▼ The small Spanish army used superior weaponry to overwhelm the Incas. They had steel swords, helmets, and armor, as well as small cannon, compared to unarmed Incan soldiers wearing leather armor.

PIZARRO'S PLIGHT

Francisco Pizarro was born into poverty in Spain sometime in the early 1470s. He never learned to read or write. He sailed on a couple of expeditions to South America before leading two expeditions to conquer the Inca Empire in 1524 and 1526. Both ended in failure. After he discovered gold and gemstones in northern Peru, he made a third successful attempt in 1532. A quarrel led to his death in 1541.

▲ Pizarro led the expedition through the Andes on the way to Cajamarca. He was a daring commander whose nerve enabled him to capture a vast empire.

▼ Despite their defeat in 1532, the Incas continued to resist Spanish rule, rising in rebellion in 1536 and fighting the Spanish until their leader was killed in 1572.

Armed to fight

The Spanish fought the Incas with crossbows, swords, and arquebuses—muskets that used a lit match to ignite the charge that shot the bullet. Above all, they had horses, animals that were unknown to the Incas. In response, the unarmed Incas fought back with stones.

CONQUERING MEXICO

About 11 years before the Spanish overwhelmed the Inca Empire, they had achieved a similar victory over another massive empire thousands of miles to the north. In 1519 Hernán Cortés set out with 600 men and 17 horses to explore the Yucatan Peninsula of Mexico on behalf of the Spanish crown. Within two years he had taken over the mighty Aztec Empire and captured Tenochtitlan, its capital city.

▼ The Aztec capital of Tenochtitlan lay on an island in the middle of the Lake Texcoco in central Mexico.

SPANISH VS. INCAS

1531	Francisco Pizarro lands at Tumbes in Inca Empire and sets off to meet Atahualpa
1532	Civil war ends in Inca Empire with victory for Atahualpa over his brother
Nov 15	Pizarro arrives in Cajamarca
Nov 16	**Pizarro's forces overwhelm the Incas and take Atahualpa hostage**
Jul 26, 1533	After the ransom was paid, Atahualpa is killed by the Spanish
1534	Pizarro enters Cuzco and controls Inca Empire

The Great Fleet

In May 1588, a large invasion fleet was ordered to set sail by Spain's powerful ruler Philip II. The Great Armada was made up of 130 ships fitted with 2,500 guns, and carried 30,000 soldiers and sailors. The ships included large warships called galleons, galleys, and supply vessels. It was headed toward England, sent to overthrow Queen Elizabeth I of England and conquer her country.

Battered ships

The Armada was first spotted off the south coast of England on July 29, 1588. On August 7, eight English ships were set alight and sent into the Spanish fleet, forcing the Spanish to cut their anchor cables and flee. The next day the two sides met off Gravelines, northern France. Five Spanish ships were sunk or captured in an eight-hour battle. The badly damaged Armada was driven northward, scattered by gales. The threat to England was over.

▼ The Spanish Armada sailed in close formation up the English Channel, attacked along the way by English ships.

▲ Elizabeth was crowned queen of England in January 1559. Although much-loved by her people, she never married.

THE ENEMY QUEEN

Elizabeth I came to the throne of England in 1558 after the death of her sister, Mary I. Mary, a Roman Catholic, had been married to Philip II of Spain. Elizabeth, however, was a Protestant and thus an enemy of Catholic Spain. Elizabeth supported the seadogs who captured Spanish treasure ships and sent support to the Dutch in their fight for independence from Spanish rule. Elizabeth ruled England until her death in 1603.

SPANISH VS. ENGLISH

1556	Philip II becomes king of Spain
1558	Elizabeth I becomes queen of England
1585	Elizabeth helps Dutch rebels fight against Spanish rule
1587	Elizabeth executes Mary Queen of Scots, a Catholic rival to her throne
April 29-30	Drake attacks Spanish fleet at Cadiz
May 28, 1588	Armada sets sail toward England
July 29	Armada sighted off the Lizard Peninsula in Cornwall
August 6	Armada anchors off Calais
August 7	England sends eight fireships to break up Spanish fleet
August 8	**Battle of Gravelines**
August 9	Wind drives Armada into North Sea
1598	Philip dies
1603	Elizabeth dies

Shipwreck!

The English pursued the Armada up the North Sea to Scotland, from where it sailed north round the British Isles and down the Atlantic Ocean to Spain. More than 50 ships were shipwrecked by storms on the Scottish and Irish coasts and at least 20,000 men lost their lives. Just 67 ships limped home to Spain.

▼ Small, fast English ships carrying long-range guns chased and defeated the large Spanish galleons.

▲ Francis Drake was knighted by Queen Elizabeth in 1581 on board his ship the *Golden Hind*, which he'd used to voyage round the world.

THE QUEEN'S PIRATE

English sailors, notably Francis Drake, regularly attacked Spanish galleons laden with gold from the New World (the Americas). In April 1587, Drake attacked the port of Cadiz and destroyed much of the Spanish fleet preparing to join the Armada. This delayed the Armada by about a year.

Brutal Battles

The Siege of
THE ALAMO

The Siege of the Alamo in 1836 did not involve large armies or result in masses of deaths. Only 189 Texan men were besieged by a force of 1,500 Mexican troops. All the defenders lost their lives, but the cause they fought for—the independence of Texas from Mexican rule—was soon achieved.

The stronghold

In 1836, as fighting between Mexico and Texas became more fierce, a group of Texan volunteers drove the Mexicans out of San Antonio, Texas, and occupied the Alamo, an old mission building. They were urged to withdraw by the Texan commander, Sam Houston, as he felt their position was too exposed. They refused.

◄ 1,500 Mexican troops advanced on the Alamo, armed with rifles and muskets.

MEXICANS VS. TEXANS

1740s	Work begins building the Alamo
1830	After U.S. migrants pour into Texas, Mexico closes the Texan–U.S. border
1835	Mexico removes rights enjoyed by Texas. Texas revolts and drives Mexican troops out of the state
Feb 23–Mar 6, 1836	**Siege of the Alamo**
March 2, 1836	Texas declares independence from Mexico
April 21, 1836	Sam Houston defeats Mexicans at San Jacinto
1845	Texas joins the U.S.

THE ALAMO'S HERO

Davy Crockett (1786–1836) is a U.S. folk hero, known to millions as the "King of the Wild Frontier." He was born in rural Tennessee and gained a reputation for storytelling. In 1826 he became a member of the U.S. Congress, but lost his seat in 1834. Fed up with his failure, he went to fight for Texan independence and was one of the men killed at the Alamo.

▶ Crockett became well known for being a strong frontiersman and soldier—and later in life, a politician.

TO THE DEATH

On February 23, a Mexican force reached San Antonio and besieged the Alamo for 13 days. In the early hours of March 6, they attacked while the Texans were asleep. The Texans soon woke and fired at the advancing enemy, but their fight was hopeless. Within 90 minutes, all 189 defenders lay dead.

▼ As the Texan defenders fired their guns over the walls, new guns were loaded behind them.

DECLARING INDEPENDENCE

While the siege of the Alamo continued, Texas declared its independence from Mexico. In April 1836, Texan commander Sam Houston defeated the Mexican army at San Jacinto. Texas then became an independent republic and remained so until it joined the U.S. in 1845 as the 28th state of the Union.

The LAST STAND

In the 1800s, the U.S. government tried to confine the Sioux to special reservations, but they continued to hunt for buffalo across the Black Hills of Dakota. As American prospectors moved into the area in search of gold, the Sioux felt threatened. On June 25, 1876, they fought back at one of the most famous battles on American soil, the Battle of the Little Bighorn.

The fatal battle

On June 25, 1876, George Custer and 210 men of the 7th Cavalry surveyed the area near the Little Bighorn River, Montana, and spotted Sioux encampments. Disobeying orders, they attacked immediately. Custer came under ferocious attack from 2,500 Sioux, who fired volleys of arrows down on them. Custer ordered his men to kill their horses and use the bodies as a barrier, but it was too late—every cavalryman was killed.

The Sioux

The Lakota and Dakota tribes of Native Americans were known as the Sioux, from the local Chippewa word for "enemy." They lived on the western Great Plains in what are now the states of the Dakotas, Minnesota, and Montana. A warlike people, they were skilled horsemen, firing arrows from their saddles with great accuracy. They carried heavy stone clubs, tomahawks or axes, and scalping knives, as well as shields for protection.

▲ For close combat, the Sioux used warclubs with a metal blade.

Warrior chiefs

Crazy Horse (c. 1840–1877) and Sitting Bull (c. 1831–1890) led their tribes during struggles with the U.S. army and white settlers. They wanted to stop them taking the Sioux land—hunting buffalo was vital to their survival—and this led to a series of battles. Crazy Horse wanted "peace and to be left alone."

◀ Sioux chief Sitting Bull led his people to victory over the U.S. Cavalry at Little Bighorn.

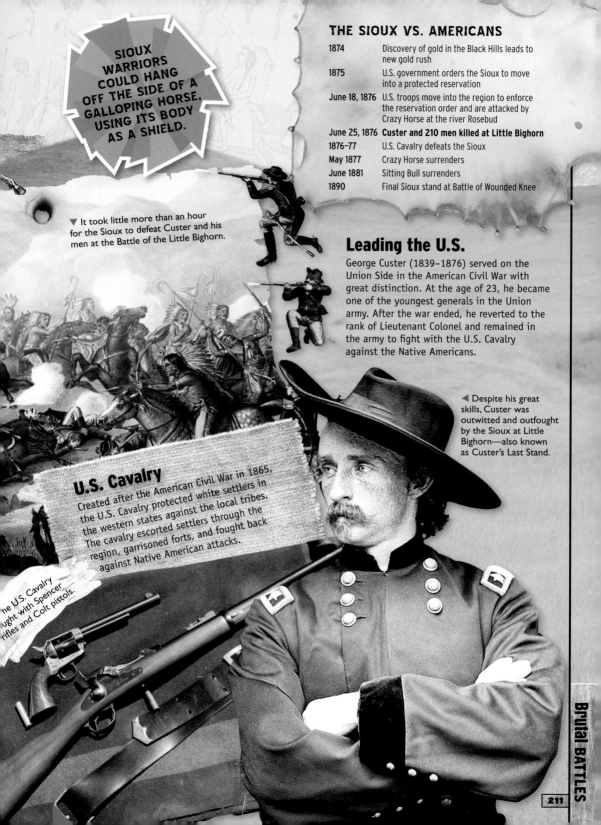

THE SIOUX VS. AMERICANS

1874	Discovery of gold in the Black Hills leads to new gold rush
1875	U.S. government orders the Sioux to move into a protected reservation
June 18, 1876	U.S. troops move into the region to enforce the reservation order and are attacked by Crazy Horse at the river Rosebud
June 25, 1876	**Custer and 210 men killed at Little Bighorn**
1876–77	U.S. Cavalry defeats the Sioux
May 1877	Crazy Horse surrenders
June 1881	Sitting Bull surrenders
1890	Final Sioux stand at Battle of Wounded Knee

SIOUX WARRIORS COULD HANG OFF THE SIDE OF A GALLOPING HORSE, USING ITS BODY AS A SHIELD.

▼ It took little more than an hour for the Sioux to defeat Custer and his men at the Battle of the Little Bighorn.

Leading the U.S.

George Custer (1839–1876) served on the Union Side in the American Civil War with great distinction. At the age of 23, he became one of the youngest generals in the Union army. After the war ended, he reverted to the rank of Lieutenant Colonel and remained in the army to fight with the U.S. Cavalry against the Native Americans.

◄ Despite his great skills, Custer was outwitted and outfought by the Sioux at Little Bighorn—also known as Custer's Last Stand.

U.S. Cavalry

Created after the American Civil War in 1865, the U.S. Cavalry protected white settlers in the western states against the local tribes. The cavalry escorted settlers through the region, garrisoned forts, and fought back against Native American attacks.

...he U.S. Cavalry ...ought with Spencer ...rifles and Colt pistols.

ZULU Power

As the British expanded their empire across southern Africa, they came into contact with the Zulus —skilled warriors whose bravery and discipline more than made up for their lack of modern weapons. In 1879 the two sides went to war.

Major defeat

In January 1879, a British army led by Lord Chelmsford invaded the Zulu kingdom. Chelmsford divided his army in two, leaving 800 British troops and 1,000 African colonial troops camped at Isandhlwana. On January 22, 20,000 Zulus attacked the camp. The slaughter was huge—more than 1,300 British and colonial troops lost their lives. The Zulus lost about 1,000 men. It was one of the worst defeats ever suffered by the British army.

▲ Poorly armed, the British troops were overwhelmed by strong Zulu forces.

◀ British troops wore striking red uniforms and carried rifles and bayonets.

British forces

The British army consisted of volunteer troops who normally served for four to eight years, with a maximum length of service of 21 years. Soldiers were paid a daily wage and were required to have a basic level of education.

Barefoot warriors

At 18 years old, Zulu boys became warriors. They fought each other in mock battles and went on forced marches and military maneuvers. In battle, they fought barefoot, throwing spears at the enemy and then attacking at close range with wooden clubs and short, stabbing spears. They never took prisoners, killing their opponents and opening their bodies to release the spirits.

◀ Zulu warriors used their shields as offensive weapons to throw their opponents off balance.

▼ A small British force heroically defended Rorke's Drift against a far larger Zulu army.

Rorke's Drift

On the evening of the main battle, 140 British troops, who were defending a nearby river crossing at Rorke's Drift, came under attack from 4,000 Zulus. The British quickly erected a barricade of wagons and grain bags and fought off the Zulus, using long bayonets against Zulu spears. The Zulus attacked all night but eventually withdrew in the morning. Only 17 British troops and 350 Zulus lost their lives. Eleven Victoria Crosses—the highest medal for valor—were awarded to the British soldiers.

BRITISH VS. ZULUS

1816	Paramount chief Shaka rules the Zulus and creates an army
Dec 1878	British issue ultimatum to Zulu king Cetshwayo requiring him to accept British rule
Jan 22–23, 1879	**British invade, but are defeated by Zulus at Isandhlwana. British hold off Zulus at Rorke's Drift**
March 1879	British suffer further defeats
July 4, 1879	Heavily reinforced British army defeats Zulus at Ulundi and ends Zulu independence

OVER
the Top

The Battle of the Somme has gone down in history as one of the bloodiest battles ever. In 1916 the British army planned to knock a large hole in the German front line near the river Somme, northern France. However, on the first day of the battle—July 1—the British suffered a catastrophic defeat.

Smashing the lines

On June 26, the British used massive artillery pieces to pound the enemy's defenses, but many of the shells did not explode. The British gunners did not realize that the Germans had rebuilt their defenses using concrete, which wasn't damaged by light shells.

▲ A British 8-in howitzer fired a 200 lb (91 kg) shell a distance of up to 31,500 ft (9,600 m).

Trench warfare

When the bombardment stopped on July 1, the Germans emerged from their safe dugouts deep underground to man the trenches and machine guns. The British troops advanced, expecting the Germans to have been killed. The soldiers were mown down by German gunfire—622 men were lost in only 10 minutes. On the first day, 57,470 British troops were killed or injured. By the time the battle ended in November, more than 1.2 million men had been killed or wounded on both sides. Neither side had gained any advantage.

BRITISH ARMY

At the start of the war, the British army consisted largely of volunteers who had signed up to fight the Germans. In 1916 they were joined by conscripts—men forced into the army. The standard weapon was the Lee-Enfield rifle, with a bayonet on the end. Soldiers used grenades and mortars against enemy trenches.

▲ Both armies dug themselves into deep, defensive trenches along the Western Front. Firing steps were built so soldiers could aim their rifles over the top without being too exposed.

IN JUNE 1917 THE BRITISH INSTALLED ONE MILLION LB (453,600 KG) OF EXPLOSIVES UNDER GERMAN LINES AT MESSINES. THE EXPLOSION KILLED 10,000 GERMANS AND WAS SO LOUD, IT WAS HEARD 130 MI (210 KM) AWAY IN LONDON.

▲ Soldiers kept their heads down when firing machine guns, as fire was immediately returned by the enemy.

Deadly shot

Both sides used machine guns to deadly effect. These guns, such as the British Vickers and French Hotchkiss, were mounted on tripods and could fire up to 450 bullets a minute. Lighter, more portable machine guns were also used.

GERMAN ARMY

Every German male, aged 17-45, took part in military service during peacetime. During the war, these conscripts became highly disciplined, effective troops. They were better educated and trained than their enemies. The Germans were the first to dig trenches, which they even equipped with electricity and piped water.

CENTRAL POWERS VS. ALLIES

Aug 1914	War breaks out in Europe as Germany invades Belgium and France. Germany, Austria-Hungary, and Turkey (Central Powers) fight Britain, France, and Russia (Allies)
Sept 1914	German advance into France halted at the river Marne
April 1915	Major battle fought at Ypres, Belgium
Feb 1916	Germans begin massive assault against French town of Verdun
July 1916	**Battle of the Somme**
July 1916	British first use tanks in battle
Sept 1916	U.S. joins war, alongside Britain and France
April 1917	Battle takes place at Passchendaele
July 1917	German advance into France
March 1918	German advance reversed
July 1918	Germans and Allies agree an Armistice to stop fighting, ending the war
11 Nov 1918	

SNIPER FIRE

The battle for Stalingrad in southern Russia marked a turning point in World War II. Until then, the Germans had defeated all before them. Now they faced a Soviet enemy determined to hold onto the city at all costs. The battle lasted for six months, with massive loss of life and a major defeat for the Germans.

OPERATION BARBAROSSA

On June 22, 1941—a year before Stalingrad—Germany invaded the Soviet Union, with an army of more than 3 million men, 3,000 tanks, and 2,500 aircraft. The Soviets were caught by surprise, and within days, their airforce had been destroyed and 600,000 troops killed or captured.

THE BATTLE OF STALINGRAD

In August 1942, 270,000 German troops attacked the city of Stalingrad. They pushed the Soviet defenders back to a narrow strip of buildings along the west bank of the Volga River. In November, the Soviets responded by surrounding the German forces. After heavy fighting, the Germans surrendered in February 1943. Around 750,000 German troops were killed or injured. The Soviets lost 1.1 million men.

▶ Thousands of Soviet troops were captured by the Germans as they advanced toward Stalingrad.

▶ Soviet troops threw grenades at German soldiers who were sheltering in the buildings of Stalingrad.

GERMANS VS. SOVIETS

Jun 22, 1941   Germany and its allies invade the Soviet Union

Sep 15, 1941   900-day siege of Leningrad (modern-day St. Petersburg) by Germans

Nov 23, 1941   Germans within reach of Moscow

Aug 19, 1942   **Attack on Stalingrad by German forces**

Nov 23, 1942   Soviet army surrounds German army at Stalingrad

Feb 2, 1943   Germans surrender at Stalingrad

THE SNIPERS

In the ruined buildings of Stalingrad, trained snipers from both sides picked off enemy soldiers one by one. The snipers even fought each other from different floors of the same building. Soviet snipers who killed 40 Germans received bravery medals and the title of "noble sniper."

▶ A rifle's telescopic sight magnifies the sniper's target.

▼ Up to 4,000 Soviet tanks took part in the battle to lift the German siege of Stalingrad.

THE CITY IN RUINS

Named after the Soviet leader, Josef Stalin, the industrial city of Stalingrad lay on the Volga River in southern Russia. The Germans were determined to capture the city named after their main enemy, while the Soviets had to defend the honor of their leader. The battle reduced the city to ruins. Every building was destroyed or seriously damaged, yet many people continued to live among the ruins. Today the city has been rebuilt, and is known as Volgograd.

▶ German soldiers patrol the ruins of Stalingrad in October 1942.

TANK Attack

I n July 1943, a major tank battle took place near the Russian city of Kursk. The Soviet army with 5,000 tanks pushed back the massive German attack of 2,900 tanks. After this victory, the Germans were driven out of the Soviet Union, until their eventual defeat in May 1945.

The Battle of Kursk

In July 1943, the front line between the German and Soviet armies ran in a "bulge" round Kursk, southern Russia. The Germans wanted to capture this bulge, but the Soviets reinforced their troops and dug massive fortifications. On July 5, the Germans attacked with 2,900 tanks and 780,000 men. In response, the Soviets had 1.4 million men and more than 5,000 tanks. The battle was so intense that the tanks often rammed each other off the battlefield.

GERMAN PANZER TANKS

At first, German tanks were superior to any enemy tank, but the sheer numbers and firepower of the Soviet T-34s eventually overwhelmed them. About 9,000 Panzer IVs were produced throughout the war.

▼ Fast and reliable, the Panzer IV was originally built as a support vehicle. It carried five crew into battle.

▼ A line of Soviet T-3[...] tanks advanced towa[...] the front line. Sturm[...] fighters in the sky destroyed any stran[...] German forces.

GERMANS VS. SOVIETS

Feb 1943	Soviet Red Army defeats Germans at Stalingrad
Jul 4–Aug 23, 1943	**Major tank battle at Kursk. Red Army wins**
Aug 1943	Red Army enters Ukraine
Jan 1944	Lengthy German siege of Leningrad ended by Red Army
July 1944	Red Army enters Poland and eastern Germany
Jan 1945	Warsaw, capital of Poland, captured by Red Army
April 1945	Red Army surrounds Berlin
May 7, 1945	Germany surrenders

The Red Army

In the first months of the war against Germany, the Soviet army were badly led and poorly equipped. They lost millions of men who were either killed or taken prisoner. As the war went on, the Soviets learned how to fight with tanks, achieving great victories against the retreating German army.

▼ Red Army troops gathered to receive instructions from their commander.

▼ At the Battle of Kursk, more than 700 tanks were destroyed in just one day.

SOVIET T-34 TANKS

The T-34 was a four-man tank—rugged, highly mobile and well protected by its armor. Designed to be mechanically simple and easy to produce, it was equipped with a tank gun and two machine guns. The first T-34 rolled off the production line in 1941. By May 1944, the Soviets were producing 1,200 T-34s every month.

INDEX

ACKNOWLEDGMENTS

publishers would like to thank the following sources for the use of their photographs:

amy B=Bridgeman CO=Corbis F=Fotolia FLPA=Frank Lane Picture Agency GI=Getty Images
stockphoto.com NPL=Nature Picture Library R=Reuters RF=Rex Features SPL=Science Photo
ry S=Shutterstock TF=Topfoto

o, b=bottom, c=center, l=left, r=right

R: Main erllre74/S, bl St. Nick/S, bc Rainer Albiez/S, br Nikolay Petkov/S
K COVER: max blain/S

IMS: 2(tr) F, 2(br) S, 3(tl) SPL, 3(bl) S, 3(tr) GI, 3(br) GI

TH'S POWER: 4–5 RGB Ventures LLC dba SuperStock/A, 6–7(c) RICHARD BIZLEY/SPL, 6(l)
D A. HARDY/SPL, 7(r) CHRISTIAN JEGOU PUBLIPHOTO DIFFUSION/ SPL, 7(tr) GlOck/S,
Picsfive/S, 8–9(b) Gary Braasch/CO, 8–9(b) Maglara/S, 8–9(bg) Roman White/S, 8–9(bg)
abo/S, 8–9(c) CHAIWATPHOTOS/S, 8–9(t) winnond/S, 8(cl) pf/A, 8(ct) RedKoala/S, 8(tl)
to/S, 8(tr) Picsfive/S, 8(tr) U.S. Geological Survey , 9(tl) oriori/S, 9(tr) Robert
linger "CMSP Biology"/N, 9(tl) monbibi/S, 9(tr) NataliSuns/S, 10 K. Miri Photography/S,
1 Elnur/S, 10(b) Alexander Paterov/S, 10(b) JIANG HONGYAN/S, 10(c) Dora Zett/S, 10(cl)
o Podor/A, 10(cr) Galaxy Picture Library/A, 11(b) DICK TESKE/EPA, 11(c) PS, 11(cr) M_G/S,
3 Philippe Hays/RF, 12(br) trekandshoot/S, 12(c) Visuals Unlimited/CO, 12(c) Raia/S,
) MarcelClemens/s, 13(br) Yves Regaldi/ZenShui/CO, 13(tc) Ashley Cooper/SpecialistStock/
shdownDirect/RF, 13(tc) Joe Gough/S, 14–15 Daniel J Bryant//GI, 14(br) NASA/SPL, 14(tl)
Wimborne/M, 14(tl) FotoSergio/S, 15(br) Imaginechina/CO, 15(tr) Tim Wimborne/R, 15(tr)
Ze/S, 16–17 Petrosg/S, 16(l) James Warwick/GI, 16(r) KARI GREER/SPL, 16(t) Sergey
nov/S, 16(tl) Hefr/S, 17(l) Frans Lanting/CO, 17(l) Lucas Dawson/GI, 17(t) Vividz Foto/S,
) AFP/GI, 18–19 KeystoneUSA-ZUMA/RF, 18–19(b) Aflo/RF, 18(bl) JOSE ANTONIO PEÑAS/
18(cr) S, 19(bc) KeystoneUSA-ZUMA/RF, 19(cr) Pakhnyushcha/S, 20–21 G.J. McCarthy/
'A, 20–21 WOLF AVNI/S, 20–21(bg) S, 20(bl) S, 20(bl) NASA/SPL, 20(t) ARENA Creative/S,
) Chad Cowan/RF, 20(tr) nuttakit/S, 21(br) mmm/S, 21(c) R, 21(c) Piyato/S, 22–23 PEKKA
TAINEN/S, 22–23(bg) StudioSmart/S, 22(bl) NASA/CO, 22(bl) Linali/S, 22(br) Chubykin
dy/S, 22(t) fluidworkshop/S, 23(br) Hamid Sardar/CO, 24–25 AFP/GI, 24(bl) Jagdish Agarwal/
24(br) 1000 Words/S, 24(l) Neale Cousland/S, 24(tl) jesadaphorn/S, 25(b) AFP/GI, 25(br)
kuliasz/S, 25(br) fotosutra.com/S, 25(br) Diana Taliun/S, 25(cl) Igor Kovalchuk/S, 25(tc)
ovao/S, 26–27 DANIEL LECLAIR/X00162/Reuters/CO, 26(bl) Liveshot/S, 26(bl) James Nielsen/
'A, 27(bl) Roxana Gonzalez/S, 27(br) Stringer Shanghai/R, 27(t) ZUMA/RF, 28–29 mdd/S, 28–
ichael Woessner/S, 28–29(bg) Scott Prokop/S, 28(br) JACK HAIJES/EPA, 28(cr) SergeyDV/S,
) JJ Studio/S, 28(cr) Lev Kropotov/S, 28(tl) Styve Reineck/S, 28(tr) KeystoneUSA-ZUMA/
8(tr) the808/S, 29(br) PABLO SANCHEZ/CO, 29(br) Andrzej Gibasiewicz/S, 29(br) ermess/S,
) Sipa Press/RF, 29(cr) Tim Burrett/S, 29(tl) Greg Epperson/S, 29(tr) Stocktrek Images/
30–31 Vladislav Gurfinkel/S, 30–31 Sundari/S, 30–31(b) PozitivStudija/S, 30–31(tc) Jose
, 30–31(bg) Daboost/S, 30(bc) Fenton one/S, 30(bc) Denys Prykhodov/S, 30(tl) DENNIS M.
ANGAN/epa/CO, 30(tr) AFP/GI, 31(bc) Asianet-Pakistan/S, 31(bc) KAMONRAT/S, 31(bl) AFP/
1(cr) ROLEX DELA PENA/epa/CO, 31(tl) Rouelle Umali/Xinhua Press/CO, 31(tr) KeystoneUSA-
A/RF, 32–33 Thirteen/S, 32–33(b) bluehand/S, 32–33(t) Binkski/S, 32–33(t) Gilmanshin/S,
) Arne Bramsen/S, 32(br) artjazz/S, 32(tr) Vasily Kovalev/S, 32(br) TrotzOlga/S, 32(cl)
eron Davidson/CO, 32(cl) Ryan Carter/S, 32(tr) Iakov Filimonov/S, 32(tr) GARY HINCKS/
33(bc) ARENA Creative/S, 33(bc) JULIE DERMANSKY/SPL, 33(br) alexsvirid/S, 33(cl) KPA/
/Rex Features, 33(cr) Iourii Tcheka/S, 33(cr) Aaron Amat/S, 33(cr) Candice Villarreal/US
/Handout/CO, 33(tr) stevemart/S, 35–36 c4dmodelshop.com, 35(bl) REED HOFFMANN/epa/
), 35(bl) Eric Nguyen//CO, 35(bl) Stephen Finn/S, 34(tr) Natykach Nataliia/S, 35(tl) GARY
KS/SPL, 36–37 Newspix/Rex Features, 36–37(bg) Claudio Divizia/S, 36(bl) CLAUS LUNAU/
37(br) DAVE HUNT/epa/CO, 37(tr) Lyndon Mechielsen/Newspix/RF, 38(bl) Zlatko Guzmic/S,
) Atlaspix/S, 38(l) Elenamiv/S, 39(bc) Jim Stem/St. Petersburg Times/WpN/PS, 39(bl) CURTIS
ETON/AP/PA, 39(br) William McGinn/AP/PA, 39(tr) c.Warner Br/Everett/RF, 39(tr) Gangster/S

DEADLY NATURE: 40–41 Design Pics Inc/RF, 42–43(b) Eric Isselee/S, 42–43(bg) Valentin
Agapov/S, 42(bl) Clivia/F, 42(bl) ULKASTUDIO/S, 42(bl) Steve Bloom, 42(cr) ArtisticPhoto/S,
42(cr) Maslov Dmitry/S, 42(tl) Steffen Foerster/S, 43(bl) Edwin Giesbers/NPL, 43(br) Antoni
Murcia/S, 43(cr) Daniel Cox/GI, 43(tl) Ljupco Smokovski/F, 43(tl) Nature Production/NPL, 43(tl)
RoyStudio.eu/S, 44–45 Jakub Krechowicz/S, 44–45 val lawless/S, 44–45(b) Noam Armonn/S,
44(b) Robert Valentic/NPL, 44(bg) Mark Yuill/S, 44(bl) SPbPhoto/S, 44(cb) gabor2100/S, 44(cr)
Nadezhda Sundikova/S, 44(l) Oariff/D, 44(t) Picsfive/S, 44(t) oksankash/S, 45(b) Yganko/S,
45(bg) Mark Yuill/S, 45(br) Jabruson/NPL, 45(br) Carlos Horta/S, 45(t) Audrey Snider-Bell/S,
46(bl) MARTY SNYDERMAN/VISUALS UNLIMITED, INC/SPL, 46(br) Norbert Wu/Science Faction/
Corbis, 46(tr) Design Pics Inc/RF, 47(b) Doug Perrine/NPL, 47(tl) EYE OF SCIENCE/SPL, 48–49
SteveUnit4/S, 48–49 zentilia/S, 48–49 Dr. Cloud/S, 48–49 Eky Studio/S, 48–49(b) Jag_cz/S,
48–49(bg) Fesus Robert/S, 48–49(bg) chaoss/S, 48(b) George McCarthy/CO, 48(tr) Pete Oxford/
Minden Pictures/FLPA, 49(b) Mark Moffett/Minden Pictures/FLPA, 49(t) Lassi Rautiainen/NPL,
49(t) Dennis Donohue/S, 50–51 Potapov Alexander/S, 50–51(bg) chalabala/S, 50(b) Massimo
Saivezzo/S, 50(bl) NHPA/P, 50(tl) Potapov Alexander/S, 50(tr) Alex Hyde/NPL, 51(bl) Nick Upton/
NPL, 51(bl) Vitaly Korovin/S, 51(br) Daniel Heuclin/NPL, 51(t) Michael & Patricia Fogden/GI,
52–53 Vividz Foto/S, 52–53 RTimages/S, 52–53(bg) khd/S, 52–53(bg) xpixel/S, 52(bc) Gary
Blakeley/S, 52(br) SJ Watt/S, 52(cr) Kevin Schafer/Minden Pictures/FLPA, 52(cr) Angelo Gandolfi/
NPL, 52(tl) RTimages/S, 53(br) Karsol/D, 53(br) Peter Betts/S, 53(cl) Clem Haagner/Ardea,
53(cl) Charidy B/S, 53(cr) borzywoj/S, 53(tc) Florian Andronache/S, 54–55(bg) Kekyalyaynen/S,
54(b) Igor Kovalchuk/S, 54(bc) Alex Wild/Visuals Unlimited/CO, 54(bc) My Good Images/S,
54(bl) Kerstin Schoene/S, 54(cl) Kletr/S, 54(cl) SmileStudio/S, 54(tl) Andrey_Kuzmin/S, 54(tr)
SCIEPRO/SCIENCE PHOTO LIBRARY, 55(bl) Dietmar Nill/NPL, 55(bl) Vitaly Korovin/S, 55(cr) JAMES
L. AMOS/NG, 55(t) Visuals Unlimited/CO, 56(bl) jps/S, 56(br) Raia/S, 56(br) Vitaly Korovin/S,
56(br) Westend61/S, 56(bl) Kovalev Maxim/S, 56(tr) Eric Isselee/S, 57(br) Raul D. Martin/
National Geographic Society/CO, 57(c) Erik Stokker/S, 57(tr) Daniel Alvarez/S, 58(bl) Lions Gate/
Everett/RF, 58(cr) NHPA/P, 58(tl) Skymax/S, 58(tl) Ronnie Howard/S, 58(tr) Jean Paul Ferrero/
Ardea, 58(tr) Picsfive/S, 59(bl) Stephen Belcher/Minden Pictures/FLPA, 59(br) Myotis/S, 59(br)
lenetstan/S, 59(br) Patryk Kosmider/S, 59(cl) Alhovik/S, 59(cl) Animals Animals/SS, 59(cr)
Courtesy of Harvard University/Handout/Reuters/CO, 59(cr) Luis Molinero/S, 59(tr) KONRAD
WOTHE/ MINDEN PICTURES/NG, 59(tr) redsoul/S, 60–61 Picsfive/S, 60–61(b) Philip Perry/FLPA,
60–61(c) Ron Austing/FLPA, 60(t) Bernd Rohrschneider/FLPA, 61(b) Luiz Claudio Marigo/NPL,
61(tl) Nelson Marques/S, 61(tr) Stu Porter/S, 62 alexvav/S, 62–63 Nataliya Hora/S, 62–63(b)
mradlgruber/S, 62–63(bg) Elenamiv/S, 62–63(c) Stefan Delle/S, 62–63(t) YKh/S, 62(bl) ROBERT
SISSON/NG, 62(br) Nature Production/NPL, 62(tr) John Cancalosi/NPL, 63(br) Matty Symons/S,
63(l) Bob Jensen/P, 63(l) Collpicto/S, 63(tr) Ingo Arndt/NPL, 64–65 blojfo/S, 64–65(bg) Dirk
Ercken/S, 64(bl) Jim Brandenburg/Minden Pictures/CO, 64(bl) Dima Fadeev/S, 64(bl) Yu Lan/S,
64(cr) NHPA/P, 65(bl) JOEL SARTORE/NG, 65(cr) NHPA/P, 65(tl) DM7/S, 65(tl) R-studio/S, 66
Picsfive/S, 67 stock09/S, 67 val lawless/S, 67 AnnPainter/S, 66–67(c) CB2/ZOB/WENN.com/N,
66–67(t) Planner/S, 66(bl) Stephanie Frey/S, 66(bl) Steve Collender/S, 66(t) Picsfive/S, 66(tl)
CB2/ZOB/WENN.com/N, 66(tr) Dr Shiyan Ho Ohba, 66(tr) R-studio/S, 66(tr) kanate/S, 67(b)
Piyato/S, 67(bl) Faiz Zaki/S, 67(bl) Faiz Zaki/S, 67(c) Earl D. Walker/S, 67(c) Korn/S, 67(cr) CB2/
ZOB/WENN.com/N, 67(c) KROMKRATHOG/S, 68(cl) Tony Campbell/S, 68(tr) Michael & Patricia
Fogden/Minden Pictures/FLPA, 69(b) LYNN M. STONE/NPL, 69(tl) Martin Zwick/NHPA/P, 69(tr)
JONATHAN PLEDGER/S, 70–71(bg) Mrgreen/D, 70(bl) Doug Perrine/GI, 70(bl) Joe Gough/S, 70(bl)
Oksana Nikolaieva/S, 70(bl) Alex Staroseltsev/S, 70(br) Winfried Wisniewski/GI, 70(br) Givaga/S,
70(cl) ivn3da/S, 70(cl) Nomad_Soul/S, 70(tl) Jaimie Duplass/S, 70(tl) Nixx Photography/S,
70(tr) Anna Henly/GI, 70(tr) Kitch Bain/S, 70(tr) Oksana Nikolaieva/S, 70(tr) Miro art studio/S,
71(bc) Vitaly Raduntsev/S, 71(bl) Lyutskevych Dar'ya/S, 71(bl) Minden Pictures/SS, 71(cl) LHF
Graphics/S, 71(cr) Julio Aldana/S, 71(cr) Nelia Sapronova/S, 71(t) Steven Kazlowski/Science
Faction/CO, 71(t) discpicture/S, 72–73 Tischenko Irina/S, 72(br) Suzi Eszterhas/Minden Pictures/
CO, 72(cl) Paul Souders/CO, 73(cl) Maridav/S, 73(br) Kathryn Jeffs/NPL, 73(cl) Doug Allan/
NPL, 73(tr) Doug Allan/NPL, 74–75 moenez/S, 74–75 S, 74–75(bg) evv/S, 74(br) Loek Gerris/
Foto Natura/Minden Pictures/CO, 74(br) Milkovasa/S, 74(br) Elliotte Rusty Harold/S, 74(cr)
imagebroker/A, 74(cr) tonyz20/S, 75(bl) ra2studio/S, 75(bl) cynoclub/S, 75(bl) age fotostock/SS,
75(c) Potapov Alexander/S, 75(tl) Handout/Reuters/CO, 75(tl) David & Debi Henshaw/A, 75(tl)
Sphinx Wang/S

WILD SCIENCE: 76–77 Al Francekevich/CO, 78–79 alexwhite/S, 78–79(bg) Bobbie Sandlin/S,
78–79(bg) Elkostas/S, 78(br) Rex Features, 78(cl) N, 79(bl) MATT MEADOWS/SPL, 79(br)
KAZUHIRO NOGI/AFP/GI, 79(t) NATIONAL INSTITUTE OF STANDARDS AND TECHNOLOGY (NIST)/
SPL, 81 mashurov/S, 80–81 val lawless/S, 80–81 kanate/S, 80–81 nikkytok/S, 80–81(bg)
Romeo1232/D, 80–81(c) Courtesy Everett Collection/RF, 80(br) Top Photo Group/RF, 80(cl)
US NAVY/S, 81(b) ZUMA/Rex Features, 81(r) kristian sekulic, 81(t) Andrey Bayda/S, 81(tr)
Loskutnikov/S, 81(tr) 123RF, 82–83 val lawless/S, 82–83 kanate/S, 82–83(bg) S_L/S, 82(bl)
Andraž Cerar/S, 82(bl) Gavran333/S, 82(br) Theodore Gray/,Visuals Unlimited/CO, 82(br) Triff/S,
82(cl) Philip Evans/Visuals Unlimited/CO, 82(cr) photastic/S, 82(cr) Surrphoto/S, 83(bl) HEALTH